# YOUR CONFIDENCE COMEBACK

# YOUR *Confidence* COMEBACK

## THE PSYCHOLOGY OF RECLAIMING YOUR POWER, VOICE, AND LEADERSHIP

DR. KASI LACEY, PHD

Streamline
BOOKS

*To the women who came before me
those who survived, sacrificed, and dreamed
before they ever knew who I would become.
You carried me in ways I will spend a lifetime honoring.*

*To my mother and grandmothers,
and to the friends who loved me as I am,
who reminded me that softness is strength
and that my voice was never meant to be quiet.*

*To the women I have coached and will coach.
Your courage, your questions, your healing,
and your hunger for more
have shaped this book as much as my own story.*

*And to my daughters, Harper Jean and Lauren Rose,
the little souls who watch me with wide eyes
and wide-open hearts.*

*May you always feel rooted in where you come from,
may you know the brilliance in who you are,
and may you walk or run through this world
owning your voice without apology.*

*You are my why.
You are my legacy.
You are the story still unfolding.*

# CONTENTS

# FOREWORD

THIS IS QUITE a book you have picked up. I don't know why you picked it, where you are in the world, in your life, or what you are uniquely hoping to gain. But what I do know is this read will be a valuable investment of your time that will pay real, tangible, point-to-the-results dividends.

How do I know? Because I've lived it. I was Dr. Lacey's (Kasi's) office "neighbor" for seven years. And all these years later, she is still a dear friend.

It is those two things, my experience as her colleague *and* friend, that allow me to share with sincerity and authenticity what you are about to encounter through her words, wisdom, and niche skill set.

It was the fall of 2011 when I applied to be a mental health therapist in Kasi's office. I interviewed in December and was hired and began working in January 2012. The interesting part of this story is that between those months, I had a baby. My first baby. A colicky, intense, non-sleeping baby. This is all to say that the bright-eyed, clear-headed, confident woman who applied for the job was not the same woman who showed up to work, just a few weeks postpartum, exhausted, and unsure of her world that had turned upside down.

Kasi hired me anyway. Not because she was desperate. But because she is particularly gifted with the vision to see in people what they may not, in the moment, be feeling themselves. She believed in me and saw the truth of who I was, even if it was presently buried. And that experience of being buoyed by her vision and encouragement has continued, unfailingly, going forward.

I don't mean to idealize her. In fact, to do so would go against who she is and what she values in herself and others. The beauty of what Kasi brings to this world is her comfort with authenticity—yours and her own. In the pages ahead, you will read about challenging, painful, and captivating moments in her life that she bravely shares because she knows her story positively impacts others. And she will challenge you to be authentic too, asking questions and considering angles, values, and choices you've never considered before.

And as tender as I could be, given that this book is written by a dear friend, I'd be remiss if I did not offer you some hard facts as well.

- Kasi is an accomplished psychologist with real-world experience in mental health strategies, confidence training, corporate psychology, mental and emotional workplace safety, and women's career strategies for advancement in position and salary.

- Your age or stage does not matter. Kasi's journey has faced the criticisms of youth and gender in a field that was exclusively dominated by older, male leadership. However, she is also significantly younger than me and many of the other women she has mentored over the years. Whether you are fighting ageism, glass ceilings, or simply trying to quiet your own internal critic, she has the experience and expertise to help you.

- I have never known her to not succeed, on her own behalf or that of others. As tender as she is, with the heart of a psychologist, she is scrappy. She has vision. And she is deeply, deeply creative. If what you want to accomplish is going to require unique strategies, patience, pivoting, writing and rewriting the script, and courage, she is a motor. She is almost indefatigable when it comes to helping others dream and then, finding a way to make it happen. If what you are looking for is someone to champion you, push you, and care for you, you have found it here.

To the many, many people whose lives will be positively impacted by Kasi's words, I'm so excited for your journey.

And to Kasi, I'm so very proud of you, happy for you, and enjoying watching you soar. Thanks for believing in me.

## ANNE RULO, LMFT, LPC
*Author, Speaker, Therapist*

# INTRODUCTION

## I'VE BEEN IN YOUR SHOES

WHEN I WAS in my thirties, I thought I had it all. A beautifully decorated corner office. A good salary with competitive benefits paired with a shiny title. A husband I adored and two beautiful girls who brightened every room they entered. It looked like the dream my younger self could only imagine and what I thought I always wanted. In fact, it's what I thought everyone wanted.

Success.

However, I also had a lot of negatives that came with it. Late nights at the office feeling like a "bad mom" for missing fleeting moments with my daughters. A team of people who helplessly watched as other leadership members berated the work they put their hearts into. And the cherry on top was working for leaders who treated me like a nuisance and overly emotional woman, rather than the competent and valuable colleague I knew I was.

The impact was unavoidable. Anxiety. Burnout. Shame. I "had it all," and yet, I was miserable. My self-confidence had been fractured, and I couldn't remember what my priorities were. After years of fighting for my dream life, I instead found myself living in a kind of twisted nightmare. As one of the few women (and previously only woman) in a position of high-level leadership,

I felt misunderstood and isolated. Out of a desire to "fit in" with the guys, I had chipped away at pieces of myself to be the person they wanted me to be.

I know now these choices were made out of self-preservation. But, that eventually led me to lose myself. After years of hiding and morphing into the person I thought my peers wanted me to be, I had become broken version of myself, crying in my nice, big office. I had the VP job, but I didn't feel respected or valued. I felt scared and alone. But, even in all this misery, it wasn't until after a nearly explosive meeting that I was forced to finally face my fears and reality.

In a moment that felt like I literally was stabbed in the heart, a boss openly berated my character, going as far as calling me a "belligerent bully." Finally, I had had enough. I was tired of the tears, stress, and hurt. I was tired of choosing everyone else, being the person I thought they wanted me to be, all the while sacrificing my needs and dreams. And it was in this moment of deep desperation that I finally allowed questions to float to the surface that I had been stifling for years.

- Am I living my best and most authentic life?
- What do I love about my life?
- Do I even like my job?
- What do I really want in this life, career, or relationship?
- Am I truly, unapologetically, happy?
- Am I living my actual purpose and making an impact on those in my world?

I had avoided these questions long enough, and as much as I dreaded their answers, I knew I needed to face reality. I couldn't keep living the way I was. My current routine was not only brutal, it was also not sustainable. The "Sunday scaries" plagued my mind and body. Each workday, I woke up anxious, I went through the day anxious, and the feeling followed me home to my family. At home, I would do my best to be the mom, wife, daughter, and friend I wanted to be. The kind of mom who wasn't stressed about tomorrow. The mom who was happy and present with her kids. But, my girls knew and saw beyond my mask. They could see the worry and exhaustion I carried with me everywhere I went. If I was hiding anything from anyone, it was only myself.

My workdays were filled with meeting after meeting and fire after fire needing to be put out. I knew my team needed me to be calm and positive, and I would be on the outside, which is a skill I learned early in childhood. However, on the inside, I was being fueled by fear, self-doubt, and worry. While trying to compete and care for everything I could flawlessly, I always felt behind when I put my head on my pillow at night. The emotionally rigorous schedule was simply not working.

Something needed to change. I needed to find myself again and embolden my voice. My kids deserved a mom who wasn't drained all the time. My staff and students deserved a leader who didn't constantly feel behind or afraid. I deserved a life filled with love, hope, excitement, not fear, scarcity, or doom. And, I had to get honest to figure out how to get there.

As I finally allowed myself to reflect on the questions that really mattered, I realized my life didn't have to be as draining as it was. My days didn't have to be riddled with anxiety, decision paralysis, and constantly trying to catch up from the day before. So, I went back to my training. With a PhD in Psychology and over fifteen years of clinical experience, I knew I needed to start to rebuild myself. I knew there was a way for me to go home at the end of the day and have energy to play with my kids. There was a way for me to go into work feeling empowered and decisive. There was a way I could look in the mirror and love the person looking back at me. There was a way for me to break free from the fears I was holding onto and live in the truth of who I was. I finally was ready to take back the reins of my life.

So, I did what I do best. I went to the experts and poured myself into reading books and articles. I listened to podcasts and essentially

Googled "how to thrive in work, life, and love." And I began reading more about what I was feeling and found out I wasn't alone. This acknowledgment of this communal experience was a game changer and shut down lies I had been fighting for a long time. I wasn't "crazy," overly emotional, or high maintenance. That whisper in my gut, the one I ignored for too long, that something had been very, very wrong, became louder and unavoidable. And that opened a floodgate.

My husband and friends rallied around me, and I let them see the broken pieces of myself that I had tried to sweep under the rug. I started sharing my internal struggles with anxiety, lack of psychological safety in the workplace, and a lifetime of body image concerns. I also happened upon a mastermind of women who were life and leadership coaches who opened my eyes to a world of possibilities and positivity. I started to reconnect to myself, remember who I was at my core, and redefine my values. In short, I started to become me again.

In tandem, I began to consider what it might look like to coach other people who were struggling in the same areas, beyond the confines of higher education or therapy. I created tools of my own to share with potential clients or anyone looking to be their most confident and authentic selves. Then, a year later, I actually bet on myself and left my VP job to pursue my dreams of having my own business and impacting the world on a larger scale.

On an important personal note, I will share that it wasn't until after I left my long-time career that I decided to reach out and find an amazing therapist to unpack all the years of fighting and trauma. I could have certainly done that before, during, or after that big career decision, but I think I was still in fight-or-flight mode and not ready. Regardless, I'm glad I did it when I was ready. Therapy has been an essential part of my healing journey.

Today, I no longer work for the organization that led with fear and scarcity. And I can confidently say I am living the dream I didn't know was possible, but was truly designed for me. As an Executive Leadership and Confidence Coach and Keynote Speaker, I now spend my days helping women and organizations learn from my personal and professional struggles, and use my background as a psychologist to help them live and work as their most authentic selves. I truly believe this is the only way to thrive.

## WHY TRUST ME?

While my education and work experience are unique to my situation, in so many ways I've been where you may be today. I've been the competent and strong woman in the room shrinking herself to fit in. The woman who has feelings and ideas, but chooses to suppress them in order to be taken seriously or avoid attention. The woman who self-rejects opportunities for jobs out of fear or imposter syndrome, even though she is more than capable and qualified to do them and more. I get it. And I've asked some of the same questions you might be asking yourself:

- Am I good enough?
- Why do I feel this way?
- How do I help my boss understand I am the best person for the promotion?
- Wait. Am I the best person for the promotion?
- What do I really want in my career and personal life?

As scary and overwhelming as these questions (or their answers!) may seem, they don't have to be. You don't have to keep surviving through cycles of burnout and anxiety. You can find freedom to be yourself whether you're alone, at work, or anywhere in between. You can feel free to stop shrinking in rooms you deserve to be in. You *can* be the woman you have always wanted to be. And I want to help you do that.

Throughout this book, I will share with you psychologically backed tools and belief systems to help you be your authentic and amazing self. We will walk together through the following topics: confidence, emotional intelligence, boundaries, people-pleasing, psychological safety in the workplace, perfectionism, work-life integration, body image, and leading with confidence.

Note: Much of the research referenced in this book (along with the experiences I share) is based in gendered terms and societal binaries. This is reflective of the current landscape of psychological and leadership research, as well as the systems in which many of us work and live. *Please know that this is not meant to be exclusionary.* If anything, it simply highlights the gaps that still exist. The gaps we must continue to close together. Because while some of the language throughout this book may follow gendered norms or traditional binaries, know this: I see you. I respect you. I honor every reader's lived experience, identity, beliefs, and choices. This book is for you. Whoever you are, wherever you come from, and however you show up in the world, I'm grateful you're here.

Additionally, while this book is written with women in mind, I wholeheartedly invite you to share it with the men in your life. For husbands, partners, brothers, sons, uncles, coworkers, mentors, and friends, these conversations are imperative. Awareness, growth, and allyship are essential pieces of the solution. A big thank you to all the men who champion equity, who lift women up, who model respect and psychological safety. This work is better, stronger, and more possible because of you.

In the chapters ahead, all the tools and lessons I share with you stem from my dedication and commitment to support and encourage other women. Equipping us to go into boardrooms and stand tall. Teaching us to take up space in rooms we are more than deserving to be in. That mission is part of why I am writing this book. The other motivation is my daughters. I don't want them to feel victim to self-doubt, held back by their gender, or by an unhealthy environment. I want more for them, and I want more for you. You deserve to live a life filled with freedom and to love yourself while doing it.

You can do this! I believe in you and all that you are. And if you are struggling, you can borrow my belief for the time being as we answer those annoying self-doubt questions and go on a journey together to find confidence in who you are.

# Chapter 1

# CONFIDENCE IS A SKILL, *NOT* A PERSONALITY TRAIT

Y EARS BEFORE I became the only woman in our upper-level leadership positions, I was a woman looking at an email informing me the vice president of my department was leaving. I learned that the search committee was actively looking to fill the position, and my heart began to race. Colleagues came by and told me I would be a great fit, encouraging me to apply for the promotion. My experience and skills exceeded what the search committee was looking for, yet I found myself doubting whether I could get, or do, the job. Questions like, "What if I'm not qualified enough?" and "Will they even take me seriously?" were constantly on my mind. But even though I felt conflicted, I have often lived by the motto, "Why not?" So, I applied and was given a phone interview.

I knew the phone interview went well, but it was followed by radio silence. While waiting to hear back from the search committee, I continued working hard at the college I loved. After a couple of weeks, the truth set in. I wasn't going to be given a second interview. Heartbreak and a blow to my self-confidence followed. And worse, I learned the rejection wasn't because of my work or ability. Even though my work, experience, and what I could bring to the table spoke for itself, the search committee was told in no uncertain words to hire a man. I was rejected because I was a woman.

Although I wish I could say I was shocked, at the time, I really wasn't. I had barely believed I deserved the position in the first place, so of course the search committee went with another candidate. Sure, they would never have picked me because I was a woman, but I felt sure it was more than that. Internally, I believed I wasn't capable. Resigned to this, I decided to stay in my position. After all, I was good at the job I had. Even though I was a little embarrassed to be passed over, my self-doubt agreed with their decision.

In the following year, I focused on growing my skills and leading my current team. And then, in a surprise exit, the recently hired VP left. The job I had doubted I was capable of but still truly wanted was back up for grabs. My heart raced thinking about it. I had a choice.

One, I could stay where I was out of fear, or two, advocate for myself. I chose the latter, harder option: advocating for myself and what I wanted. The previous interview, the rejection, and the year of growth had changed me. I wanted to do what I knew I could. I could not forget the carrot of possibility dangled in front of me. I knew I could be a successful, compassionate, and effective VP. The challenges the department and students faced at the college were not scary or daunting to me. I knew what needed to be done, and, this time, I had developed the confidence to be sure I was the right person for this job. I decided that ultimately the job came down to relationships, and I was exceptional at cultivating and maintaining relationships. Yes, the pay raise and title were exciting, but they were more perks than motivators. I wanted my seat at the table, the chance to make a difference, and to make my own legacy. I was ready to do what the other VPs couldn't do: succeed.

Pushing through the pain of previous rejection and now confident in who I was—a more than competent employee who went above and beyond the expectations for the role—I fought for the job. Without cowering, I went to the President of the college, and I told him why I was the best fit and candidate to be the VP. It was difficult, uncomfortable (truly felt like I might throw up), and at the same time freeing. Finally, I was being myself, and I loved it. In tandem, so did the President, and I was appointed interim VP! In short order, after a couple of months of hard work and success, I was offered the permanent VP role. It felt like an incredible victory! I had finally climbed the mountain and claimed my title and victory, or so I'd thought.

At the time of my promotion, I became one of two women VPs. A few months later, the other female VP left, and I was the only female VP (and youngest) for many years to follow. This unique combination of gender and leadership at the college forced me to answer new questions. Was I going to shrink, or was I going to boldly be myself? Was I going to believe the lies I was fed, or was I going to believe I was qualified and deserving of what I wanted? Was I going to be afraid, or was I going to be confident? And what exactly did it look like to do any of this? These are the types of questions we'll explore.

## WHAT DOES "BE CONFIDENT" MEAN ANYWAY?

Go ahead and raise your hand if someone has ever looked at you and said, "Just be confident." What does that even mean? When I think about that advice, my first response is simple: Of course, I want to "just be confident," but how do I do it? What are the steps? Sometimes, confidence is presented as some elusive character trait certain people are just born with. In reality, confidence is a skill, one you must learn and practice. Admittedly, I've had to actively work on my confidence at various points throughout my life. And while I feel confident most days now, it has not always been that way. It is a process.

To start being more confident, I first had to become aware of the lies I was believing. I had to confront lies I had been told about who I was and replace them with the truths of who I wanted to be. Because while my promotion was a growth moment in this area, later I would end up having to stand up for myself on a grander scale, a story we will come back to later. As women, we get a lot of advice about what we "should" be (i.e., confident), but rarely does that result in the practical steps to figure out what we truly need.

# THE LIES WE RECEIVE AND BELIEVE

Historically, women have been raised to be in community and to be keenly aware of others. This communal mindset can be helpful in teaching empathy, understanding, and sensitivity early on in a girl's life. And while it isn't inherently wrong to raise girls to be aware of others' feelings and lives, it can be a slippery slope. Being surrounded by your peers can be encouraging. Seeing your friend hired at their dream job, marry their seemingly perfect partner, or succeed at something they have been working at for years can be a joyous celebration for you both. However, another's success can also lead to uncomfortable questions within yourself.

- Why haven't I been promoted yet? I've been working just as hard.
- Why am I not married? Do I want to get married? Have kids?
- When will I get to buy the house, travel where I want?
- Why can't I be happy and have it all too?
- What am I doing wrong? What is wrong with me?

If you have asked these questions, you are not alone. I have felt the same way many times. It is nearly impossible not to compare ourselves to other people, and specifically to the other women in our lives. Because we are raised to be aware of each other, we have heightened emotional intelligence, increasing our connectedness with one another's experiences. Of course, feeling ashamed of wanting something someone else has won't fix the problem (but it also doesn't make us a bad friend or person!). Constantly comparing ourselves to the people around us will never make us more confident. It will only keep us feeling hopeless. Asking ourselves, "Why don't I have what they do?" keeps us feeling insufficient. Instead, we need to learn to work through it productively. And, to work through comparison, there must first be an awareness of what it is we are comparing.

## COMPARE TO DESPAIR

Let's imagine a scenario. Anne is in her mid-thirties and is working just outside of her dream field. She shows up every day, works hard, and is the definition of a team player. After work one day, Anne hops on social media. Her friend Nicole just got a job in Anne's dream field. Anne texts Nicole, congratulating her and mentioning they must catch up soon. However, following her initial joy for Nicole, Anne finds herself on the verge of tears. Jealous tears. Her gut reaction is to feel both shame and anger. Shame for feeling jealous of Nicole and anger for being in the job she is in. Let me be clear. Anne is not a bad person. And she isn't a bad friend. She is simply a person who is feeling the initial despair caused by comparison. Anne has a few options to manage what she is feeling.

A.  She can push down what she is feeling and pretend like everything's fine.
B.  She can bury herself in work, trying to compete with Nicole.
C.  She can explore why she is feeling the way she is after seeing Nicole's promotion.

Option C is certainly the most productive, but where do you tend to start? Being honest about our gut reactions and coping mechanisms is one of the first steps towards growth.

This page marks the first time we will pause and allow you an opportunity to seek growth and understanding in your own journey. Grab a sheet of paper and take a moment to remember a time when you felt like Anne. Confused. Jealous. Uncomfortable. Then answer the following questions:

- What do/did they have that I want?
- Why do/did I want what they have?

Acknowledging the hurtful thoughts and feelings that comparison brings to your mind is paramount to finding the root of your despair. To address a problem, you must confront it. This may seem scary, like opening Pandora's box, not knowing how you're going to close it. However, finding out why you feel the way you do is one of the necessary steps to help lead you out of the darkness of comparison and into confidence.

## COMPARE TO AWARE

Now that you know what you want, you can say it with confidence. This is one step closer to securing what you want. The next steps are recognizing why you were triggered, setting healthy boundaries, and affirming the good things you want.

In our example scenario, Anne might be asking herself, "Why does Nicole's promotion bother me?" She knows she wants something Nicole has, but now what? How does she avoid being negatively affected by Nicole's success? It is also important for Anne to get specific here on what exactly she is feeling jealous about: Is it the title, raise, flexible work schedule, or job itself that she finds appealing? Often, once we look closely, we can better understand what exactly it is that is fueling our jealousy and comparison. Once Anne recognizes specifically *why* Nicole's success bothers her, she can move on in a healthy way toward achieving her own goals. This practice helps us realize that our reactions are not really about another's success but instead, our own inner desires.

Another strategy that can help us with comparison is to set boundaries around influences that trigger comparison. Anne saw Nicole's promotion on social media. Anne could mute Nicole's posts. She could take a social media break for a little bit or forever. I used to give this advice to my clients who recently went through a breakup: "If it makes you feel badly, stop looking at his or her social media. Stop allowing the emotional cutting." You will need to decide your boundaries and what you need in these moments. And it's okay to need them. *Strength is not always found in taking the hardest path.* As time goes on, your boundaries may change, and that is more than okay.

Whether it is a post, something someone said, or even seeing a billboard in the middle of nowhere, we can all experience triggering automatic thoughts. However, it is vital to remember: thoughts are not facts. And while the thought may trigger an emotion, we do not have to internalize every emotion we have. Hard emotions do not have to dictate our confidence. Instead, they can serve as curious sources of information, helping us better understand ourselves and our wants.

Now, once we understand what we want, we can affirm those desires instead of feeling ashamed of them! One practical way to do this is to start a dream journal. And it is exactly what it sounds like . . . writing down what you want to give you clarity on your path. Research suggests you are far more likely to achieve something if you physically write it down. I have experienced for myself the power of visualization and I write down my dreams as if they have already happened. In fact, I am going to do that right now. "I am a successful, published author."

Now your turn. Take a slip of paper or go to your preferred app to write down what you want. As women, sometimes we do not take the time to get quiet, ask, and *listen* to ourselves. Take the time to ask yourself questions like "How am I feeling?" and "What do I really want?" Once you ask yourself these important questions, apply the answers to your personal, professional life, and/or relationships. Follow up the identification of your goals and desires by writing down positive characteristics about yourself and affirming your wants. Note: Do not be afraid to dream big, even outlandishly here. If it feels uncomfortable, that is okay. Audacity and discomfort are the keys when writing down our dreams. Desires placed on our hearts are there for a reason, and as we affirm and honor them, it helps us stop self-rejecting and shooting down our own dreams.

In practice, Anne might engage in this exercise by writing down that she wants a promotion, raise, new title, car stipend, or work from home on Fridays. She can follow those desires by writing down reasons she is more than qualified, with her years of experience and education, to ask for some or all of these things. Maybe for you, it is a certain relationship, career, or dream home. It is different for each of us. These first two steps of working through comparison—recognizing despair and becoming aware—are mostly internal, but it is our internal work that later leads to external expression.

## COMPARE TO DARE

After all that internal processing, now it's time to take what you want and make it a reality. Take some time now to ask yourself the following:

- What do I need to do to achieve this/these desire(s)?
- Am I ready to change what I am doing now to achieve the future I want?
- What limiting beliefs or old identities do I need to let go of to make this dream or goal a reality?

While working through these questions, it is important to keep the possibility voice in your head, "What I want is possible." If Nicole can be promoted at work and get a position in her dream field, so can Anne. You can also take practical steps to reinforce your internal process. As an example, Anne could reach out to Nicole, ask about her experience, and learn more about out how she got the promotion. Here is the thing: Most problems are "figureoutable"; we just have to be willing to look for answers.

*Success always leaves clues*, and we just have to be brave enough to look, listen, and ask others who have what we want. You can achieve what you want. Even if the way your friend was promoted, got engaged, or traveled feels unattainable, it doesn't mean you can't do those things. Your journey just may look different than theirs. As I write this, I know it is hard to always believe you can and do deserve it, but I promise you do. Again, I am happy to lend my belief in you for the time being until you embody it for yourself.

## NAMING YOUR INNER CRITIC

Let's talk about one of the most destructive things that gets in our way when trying to achieve our goals. Our inner critic. It's the voice in our heads telling us, "You'll never be good enough." A hater of self-confidence and a hater in general, the voice is so loud and convincing at times, that it may seem like our inner critic knows us best. And, in truth, in some ways it does. It is our inner critic who knows our deepest secrets, most embarrassing moments, and greatest fears for the future. It knows how to make us feel small and breakable. It knows how to hurt us where only it can via the core fears of who we are. But it doesn't know all of who we are and more importantly it does not dictate our future and who we can become.

The truth is that you are more than your fears and limiting beliefs. The fearful thoughts in your mind do not equal the complete truth of who you are. You are more than the inner critic will ever acknowledge because it only feeds on the negative.

So, how do you silence the voice in your head fueled by fear? First, you name it. Mine is named Cassie, because she's an ASSie. Cassie has been with me as long as I can remember. She was there when I didn't get the initial VP promotion. She told me it was because I wasn't good enough and I never would be, despite all of my previous accomplishments. In addition, Cassie is well acquainted with my unstable and hectic upbringing, which is a large influence on any of my negative thinking patterns. She knew about the constant moves instigated by my mom's ever-changing choices and my uncomfortable experience as the perpetual new kid. The girl who strived to be loved by her divorced and divided parents, the "golden child" who made good grades, and the one who felt like she never really fit in because of her unapparent biracial identity. It was a lot, and she was there for it all.

She was also there when I was applying for college, telling me I would never be able to get into the schools I wanted (especially as a sixteen-year-old girl who moved out on her own). She told me I didn't deserve it because I wasn't rich enough or smart enough. She was really unkind to me about my body and weight. She was wrong over and over again, but I have slowly learned over the years not to give her voice power over me. Cassie isn't Kasi.

Just as I do with Cassie, when you name your inner critic, you take power from it. A friend of mine named her inner critic "Steve" because she would never let a man talk to her the way her inner critic did. When you name it, you can start telling it to leave you alone. As we discussed with comparison, you must become aware of what your inner critic is saying to you. Pushing it down isn't going to make it go away. Addressing this voice will help you learn why those fears feel so daunting or even at times debilitating. Then, once you've turned down the volume of your inner critic, you make room for its antithesis. The Best Friend Filter. The Best Friend Filter is the ultimate hype woman: She cheers for you, loudly, unapologetically. I refer to mine as Coco Confidence (because your girl loves some Chanel). She is luxurious, does not have time for haters, knows her worth, and is a classy queen. I envision her turning down her nose at negativity. While the inner critic points out your flaws, the Best Friend Filter points out your strengths. It is fueled by love, not fear.

On an important side note, while we do want to turn down the volume on our inner critic, what we don't want to do is villainize it. In fact, I like to try to look at my inner critic, "Cassie," from a place of love. While she is annoying, I believe she exists to protect me and, for the most part, means well. Her job is rooted in that part of my brain that wants to keep me safe from danger or exchanges with a toxic person. Our brains are wired for protection, not positivity. That means that we have to train our minds to look for the good, say confident, and choose belief over fear. I often realize that "Cassie" just needs a nap or maybe a Snickers. (Lack of sleep and hunger are gasoline for Cassie's engine.)

When we are in the moment, doing great things, it can be hard to remember all the things we are doing "right" but instead allow our inner critic to make us focus on what we could be doing better. It's part of being human. Who doesn't want to grow past their flaws and into a better person? Except maybe someone with Narcissistic Personality Disorder, but I would bet they are not reading this book. The problem is when we allow our inner critic to disregard the good things we do. So, how do we encourage our Best Friend Filter to speak more often and with more volume? Here are some strategies.

## THE BRAG BOOK

In addition to the above internal work, there are also external practices you can implement into your day to retrain your brain to focus on the positives. Here's your first strategy. Get yourself a brag book. This will help you see what you've done, all that you have accomplished, and identify when your inner critic is telling you lies. When your inner critic says, "You are useless and have not done anything today," you can go to your brag book and tell your inner critic, "Stop! I am not useless. See what I have done!" Your brag book is specific to you, like mine is specific to me. However, there are a couple of core tenets I recommend for every brag book.

### Just Start Somewhere!

You don't need to buy a new notebook or fancy pens to start. (However, I do love pretty office supplies, so if that's your thing, go for it.) It can be as simple as writing your accomplishments in your notes app, on a scrap piece of paper, or in an email to yourself. Just start. Take five minutes to remember what you've done this past week. You deserve to remember your successes.

## Recognize Your Wins, Both Big and Small

Some days you will be celebrating finishing a big project like cleaning out that closet, and other days you will be celebrating those fifteen minutes of peace you got showering while your kids played with the dog. It's important to include things we tend to dismiss as just "life." Remembering to write that check, make that appointment, or get your hair cut are wins! Take time to write down all kinds of wins: personal, professional, small, big, or even funny.

## Check In with Yourself

I check in with myself very intentionally on an annual basis. Each year, I take some time to look back and audit all that I've accomplished. It goes without saying, but a lot can happen in a year. In fact, so much can happen that we often forget things. The big moments easily eclipse the small ones and may leave us feeling even smaller. For example, one of my biggest wins ever was getting my PhD (at the age of twenty-six). It was a huge accomplishment, but I also wrote hundreds of papers. I spent hours in clinicals and read more books than I knew could be written about my thesis. I also did all this work while navigating difficult situations, and life was "life-ing." Those lead-up and behind-the-scenes accomplishments matter too. What accomplishments have you had where you may have dismissed the value of the "small" moments along the way?

Reminding yourself of the more complete picture of what you've done encourages self-confidence. Reading your brag book, especially on those difficult days, can be the best medicine for self-doubt because it allows acknowledgement to meet gratitude. When we take the time to appreciate what we have done, we offer ourselves credit instead of doubt. And when we review these "brags" with our future dreams and desires in mind, we are more likely to remember we are the person for that promotion or opportunity and see it with our own eyes.

In this journey toward who you are and what you want, it is important to start bringing that same person you want to be into every part of your life. Stop sending your "representative" to meetings or even dates. Stop outsourcing the decisions in your personal or professional life. You are the expert on your life, the only person who can be you, and that is something to celebrate. (Feel free to add this as your first brag: "I am the expert of my life.")

# Chapter 2

# PEOPLE-PLEASING ISN'T A PLEASANT LIFE

WHEN I STARTED as the interim VP, my oldest daughter was entering her "fun" toddler years as I clumsily navigated motherhood and my new leadership role. To my surprise, my interim role was short-lived. Due to my success and advocating for myself, I was quickly appointed to the permanent position only a few months later. Everything was going great, until the college announced new interim senior leadership would be implemented: a changing of the "guard." At this point in my career, I had become very acquainted with leadership turnover, but this time was different. It was also the spring of 2020, and the entire world flipped upside down with the COVID-19 pandemic bringing on one of the biggest challenges in my career to date. The emergency plan from the new leadership stated my position was to serve as the point person and chair of the pandemic task force. Y'all, I'm a psychologist: not a pandemic or disease specialist. But, true to form, I said, "Sure, I can do that!"

Naturally, the new leadership wasn't the first thing on my mind. I felt the weight of the world on my shoulders. I wanted to make the "right" decisions to protect the health and safety of our students, faculty, staff, and community members. I also wanted to make the "right" business decisions that wouldn't bankrupt the college. Tirelessly, I researched innovative practices, put together committees, consulted with experts, and did my best to organize an effective and safe plan for everyone involved. And, more often than not, I emphasized every plan expires at midnight as we would regroup with new and pertinent information each day.

Like many other parents during COVID-19, I did much of this while working from home, with a toddler. One time, I was leading a call with executives and board leadership (a majority of whom were older men) while watching my daughter alone. I will never forget hearing, "MOM, I POOPED," clear as day coming from the baby monitor. Every day brought its own unique and exhausting challenges.

Since my husband was in law enforcement, he had an "essential worker" title. Therefore, he often wasn't home as I navigated early motherhood and leadership. To say this was a difficult season, personally and professionally, is an understatement. But we made it through. During those challenging days, my leadership skills shined as I have always been effective at bringing people together, assessing situations, and making informed decisions. I used my training and skills as a psychologist to navigate the spectrum of perspectives ranging from "We are all going to die" to "This is a hoax and COVID-19 isn't real."

After successfully navigating the pandemic, it felt natural to be given additional responsibilities related to community relationships, strategic planning, and diversity, equity, and inclusion. To most, I was "thriving" in my career (or at least that is what it looked like on the outside and on paper). At this time, I strategically negotiated a long overdue raise in my salary and felt like I had finally made it into the coveted inner circle. Even though it was a good ol' boys club, it felt like I somehow found the secret back-alley entrance.

## TRAGEDY DOESN'T FOLLOW A CONVENIENT TIMELINE

Then came our family tragedy. My mother-in-law (Mimi) was diagnosed with stage 4 cancer. Our weekends quickly turned into traveling back and forth between home, doctor's appointments, treatments, scans, and everything else in between. Within eight months of her diagnosis, she passed away.

While we did our best to make and treasure every moment we had with her, it was an incredibly emotionally taxing time for all of us. But there is a silver lining to this story. Then, a month after her passing, we were surprised with a positive pregnancy test (we'd been trying for another child for many years). I truly believe our daughter was the gift that Mimi left behind, so we gave our daughter her name in honor of the fierce, funny, motivated, and strong person that was my five-feet-two-inches-tall mother-in-law.

An added layer to the story is, right before my pending maternity leave, that interim leadership was appointed permanently to their positions. To a degree, this was exciting. It brought stability to many roles and facets of the college. On the other hand, as a young female in leadership, I was in the minority and going on maternity leave brought on its own anxieties and fears. I was worried that if I took too much time off, I would be disconnected from work and left behind on projects or opportunities. To combat my fears, I chose to people-please. I only took six weeks of maternity leave and Zoomed into as many meetings as possible during those six weeks.

When I returned to work, I was ready to see what I'd missed. I was curious what had changed, and I was hopeful the changes were for the better. Unfortunately, I didn't love what I saw. Instead of an uplifting team, I noticed certain members were openly belittled by the new leadership. If individuals made minor mistakes, forgot small details, misunderstood a directive, or even decided to leave due to the toxic environment, the reaction was less than supportive. I was shocked, and I didn't want to end up like my coworkers. My automatic response was to start people-pleasing to survive. It had worked when I was little. So, I assumed it would work now.

# EARLY COPING & SURVIVAL STRATEGIES

I grew up with two divorced parents who lived in different states. While my mom moved my brother and I around the Midwest during the school year, we lived in Texas with my dad during the summers. It was the only time of year that I would spend quality time with my dad, and I wanted to make it count. I wanted him to be proud of me. I wanted to be a "good girl." So, when my dad asked me to do anything I would. As a young girl, I lived out the belief that people-pleasing my dad would make him love me.

Over the years, these people-pleasing tendencies snowballed. They became my go-to methods to feel safe and loved. At the time, I would've thought I was just being a respectful daughter, but this pattern bled into other areas of my life and relationships. I subconsciously believed my acceptance hinged on others' perception of me, my ability to make others happy, and saying yes to any request. Like, of course, you can take my car, I'd be happy to do your homework for you, and, sure, I'll pay for dinner. It took me many years to realize I was acting as a people-pleaser and this behavior was problematic and unsustainable.

It took me a long time to recognize this trait in my own behavior, because I often conflated kindness with people-pleasing. Sometimes it can be hard to know if you are living life as a people-pleaser, but the key component is to reflect on *why* you say yes. Here are a few questions you can start to ponder:

- Do you say yes when you want to say no?
- Do you resent the people you help?
- Do you struggle with feeling exhausted after being "nice"?
- Do you avoid conflict at any and all costs?
- Are you fearful someone will be mad or disappointed in you if you don't help them?

If you answered yes to any of these questions, you are exhibiting people-pleasing tendencies. Being a people-pleaser doesn't mean you are an evil or manipulative person. At its core, people-pleasing stems from a desire to experience safety, connections, and acceptance. It isn't wrong to want to feel safe, but being a people-pleaser will never bring you long-term safety—only short-term satisfaction.

| Short-Term Satisfaction of People-Pleasing | Long-Term Effects of People-Pleasing |
| --- | --- |
| Temporary peace in relationships | Loss of identity |
| Receiving external validation | Damaged self-worth |
| Avoiding conflict | Burnout |
| Feeling indispensable | Anxiety |

To honor who we truly are, we must replace fearful people-pleaser responses with healthy responses grounded in self-love and freedom.

When working at the college, I had done everything right. I showed up early. I worked late-night events. I wrote flawless reports. I connected with the students, and they enjoyed my leadership style. And while I was a great VP, that didn't stop my people-pleasing behaviors. All I had accomplished while living as a people-pleaser only affirmed my fears. If I set firmer boundaries or stopped going above and beyond, I believed I would no longer belong, be accepted, or be loved. So, the deeper I went into my career, the deeper my people-pleasing tendencies took root. They also gave life to my chameleon tendencies, which we will talk more about in the next chapter. That's the thing about operating as a people-pleaser. It feeds more bad habits. Here are just a few:

- Perfectionism
- Over-functioning
- Conflict avoidance
- Suppressing emotions
- Over-apologizing
- Imposter syndrome

## WHAT EXACTLY DOES IT MEAN TO BE A PEOPLE-PLEASER?

People-pleasers aren't born. They're often created from chaotic, unpredictable, and psychologically unsafe environments. In my case, I was taught to be a people-pleaser from a young age. Since my mom was constantly moving my brother and me all over the Midwest, I had to learn how to adapt to the chaos. As an eight-year-old, I wouldn't have been able to put into words how I wanted to feel a sense of belonging, acceptance, and likability, but it's what I wanted. When I was a "good girl" or lived within the golden handcuffs of people-pleasing, I was able to secure those results. For a time, I would feel like I belonged, was accepted, and was liked by my peers.

When I was little, I didn't know how long I would be living in the house we were currently in. I didn't know if I would be packing up my stuffed animals in a few months or even a few weeks. So, people-pleasing created a kind of home within myself. It wasn't a literal four walls, but it gave me the sense of control and certainty that I was desperately seeking. If my teacher asked for a student to help with a task, I knew I would feel accepted if I helped out. Even if the task was something I hated doing, I was willing to, because I wanted to belong. I even remember volunteering to babysit my teachers' kids, even though at the time I was not a fan of kids (they still scare me a little, even though I have two of my own). I vividly recall that night, having no clue what I was doing, and watching the clock move at an unnaturally slow pace. But I wanted my teacher to like me.

As a kid, this didn't seem like a bad thing. My teachers liked me (even if they never asked me to babysit again). My mom said she was proud of me. I was able to make friends at every school I transferred to. However, as an adult, the people-pleasing tendencies yielded different results. When I would people-please at work, my bosses wouldn't give me a gold star. Instead, they would continue to expect more from me. I would make it look easy, doing more with less, while inside overwhelmed, not wanting to show my true feelings because I believed sharing my discomfort would only prove I was not capable and also burden others with my feelings. I would then come home exhausted, which affected how I interacted with my family. People-pleasing is how I responded when my safety felt threatened. It was my response to the trauma of instability that I experienced that helped me feel safe.

## TRAUMA RESPONSES

While your experiences may vary greatly from mine, very few of us go through life without experiencing some kind of traumatic experience. And each of us reacts to fear and trauma differently. The three most common trauma responses are fight, flight, and freeze. Each of these trauma responses is rooted in some kind of feeling. If you feel angry, enraged, or confrontational, you might want to react with a fight response like yelling at the person associated with those feelings. If you feel anxious, panicked, or avoidant, you might react with a flight response such as physically leaving a room. If you tend to shut down or feel numb, you may act with a freeze response, like staring at the floor until the situation has subsided. And while these were the most recognized trauma responses for many years, psychologists have recently added the fawn response, which is tied to the freeze trauma response.

The fawn response is when people will follow a person who seems to be able to appease the current threat regardless of how healthy that may be. For example, someone blindly does everything their manager tells them to do even if it's outside their scope to avoid the wrath of a supervisor. You agree to be on that committee, even though you are completely drowning at work. Any power dynamic further complicates a threatening situation. Professionally, it is especially complicated when there is conflict between an employee and their boss or direct supervisor. I would know. I lived through these situations.

One time, I was in a meeting, and I corrected an item on the agenda. It was a simple correction that needed to be said for accuracy's sake. One of my bosses responded by passive-aggressively leaving me out of future meetings for multiple weeks. He even went as far as to ask a student to tell me I wasn't invited to a student-led meeting. The truth I learned too late was this: No amount of people-pleasing would make someone respect me. While I was saying yes to just about every request from him, I was subsequently saying no to other things I wanted to do, like spending more time with my family, going to the gym, or investing in my staff. People-pleasing holds you back from living the life you want to live. Instead, you're living the life your boss, partner, friends, or family wants you to live and possibly not getting the safety and respect you want anyway.

## THE WORLD KEEPS SPINNING

Life is full of opportunities. However, only sometimes does life offer you good opportunities when it is convenient. Recently, a colleague of mine asked if I would be interested in sitting on a board. It was a wonderful opportunity to work alongside people who were doing work I believed in. The people-pleaser in me wanted to immediately say, "YES!" But, at this point, I had finally done enough work to silence the people-pleaser and amplify my own voice. I had to weigh my options.

| Pros | Cons |
| --- | --- |
| Sitting on the board could broaden my connections. | I already have very limited time. |
| I would have the opportunity to champion a cause I believe in. | I might miss out on opportunities to invest in my family's lives. |
| It would make me feel good to serve in my community. | I was already actively involved in serving members in my community. |
| It would make my colleague happy if I said yes. | Saying yes to this opportunity meant saying no to opportunities I wanted more. |

In the end, my answer was, "No." And guess what? I'm still friends with my colleague, the board is still active, and the world keeps spinning. When I chose to embolden my voice and act according to my most important values, I allowed myself to invest my time in what I most wanted to do. Instead of going to early morning meetings, I gave myself the option to drive my kids to school or actually attend my daughter singing or reading in school. Instead of networking with a group of people I already felt fairly acquainted with, I was able to go to events where I was able to meet new colleagues in my current field. It was the right decision for me at the time. Maybe you are looking at a similar situation or have encountered one in the past. Regardless, as you begin to practice the principles we have discussed in this book, you will certainly need to practice this type of decision making at some point.

Grab a piece of paper and identify a previous situation where someone asked you to do something. It could be a workplace situation like mine, or a simple request from a family member. Split the paper into two columns and work through a pro/con list.

Do you agree with the answer you gave at the time, or do you disagree with your former self? If you disagree with the decision you made, don't sweat it. While we can learn from our previous decisions, it's imperative to look back with love and curiosity rather than condemnation. You made the best decision you could at the time with the information you had. It's okay. You'll have more opportunities to say "no" in the future. I'm sure of it.

# THE ROAD MAP BACK TO YOU

Let's take a look at Gina. She has been working at the same company for five years. In that time, she has had multiple managers. And each of the managers she's had quit within two years of their start date. While they said they quit to pursue other career options, she knows the truth. The director, Madison, was known to be more of a bully than a boss. Additionally, since Gina has been at the company, she has started going to therapy. After a few sessions, she learned that she has been choosing to be a people-pleaser over being true to herself. She knows she needs to make a change. If I were Gina's confidence coach or therapist, I would walk her through the following road map to leave people-pleasing in the dust.

## STEP 1—NOTICE

Since people-pleasing is often a long-established habit, Gina needs to learn to clearly identify her people-pleasing tendencies so she can know what people, conversations, or actions trigger her. I would tell her to walk through a day or week of her life while asking herself the following:

- When were moments she felt she needed to engage in people-pleasing?

- What was she hoping would come out of this people-pleasing behavior, or what was she trying to avoid?
- Who was involved in those situations?
- What emotion was she feeling in those moments?

I would also encourage her to write down those interactions in either her journal or on a piece of paper she can reference later.

## STEP 2—NAME

After you identify your people-pleasing tendencies, you have to start naming what you want. For Gina, she was given the opportunity to name what she wanted when her director asked her to work an after-hours event. In that moment, Gina wanted to say, "No problem, Madison!" However, she knew she had a previous commitment outside of work on the same night. She didn't want to work the after-hours event and she would be sacrificing something else she wanted to do. It was time to implement step two of the road map. She needed to put into words what she really wanted and claim it. She could either . . .

A. Say yes to her director and adjust her plans.
*Or*
B. Say no to her director and go to her previous commitment.

Let's assume Gina decides she is going to go to her previous commitment. Now, she must choose *how* she is going to say "no," or if she needs to set a firmer boundary with her director. She might use one of these options below.

A. Thank you for the invitation. Unfortunately, I have a prior commitment and won't be able to attend.
B. I appreciate you including me. I already have another obligation at that time, so I won't be able to make it this time.

C. Thank you for thinking of me. I'm not available due to a previously scheduled commitment, but I'd be happy to follow up afterward or stay in the loop.

If you're stuck in a people-pleasing mindset, it can be difficult to hear you say your own wants and desires regarding a particular situation. But when you have the courage to name and claim a situation, you're taking control over your life and reclaiming agency over your decisions. You're able to silence the internal people-pleaser and affirm your decision when you make it yours.

## Step 3—Challenge

Since being in therapy, Gina has been able to pinpoint when she started feeling bad about telling people "no." Now, she is being faced with an opportunity to challenge those feelings for the better. Gina isn't being selfish, rude, or a bad employee. She has every right to tell Madison, "No." As scary as it may feel to tell someone no, remember the possibility(ies) of what you are saying yes to. For Gina, saying no to Madison opens her life to say yes to multiple opportunities.

- She can go to her previously scheduled event.
- She doesn't have to rearrange her work schedule to make room for a task that doesn't fall under her desires or capacity.
- She is less anxious than she would be if she had said yes.

Remember, "no" is a full sentence. When you say no, you don't have to elaborate or help the other person understand why you said no. It's completely your choice, and you don't owe the asker a reason. You are in control of your life. This doesn't mean you have to be a jerk when you tell someone no, but you should feel the confidence not to explain, especially over-explain yourself.

## Step 4—Practice

As with most things, practice makes you better. The same goes for reducing your people-pleasing tendencies. If you're out of practice listening to what you truly want and then advocating for it, you will need to practice. For Gina, I would encourage her to start by saying no where she feels safe. She could start by standing in front of the mirror and rehearsing. She can practice what she might say if someone asked her to do something she didn't want to do. As she feels more confident, she could reach out to a trusted friend. Gina could ask her friend to sit with her so she can practice saying no.

As silly as you might feel "practicing" communication, there is no shame in asking for help. Gina needs to build her "no" muscle. The more comfortable she becomes with even physically saying the word no, the easier it will be for her to use it in real-time. The same goes for anyone who is trying to stop people-pleasing. "No" isn't your enemy. It's an ally to help protect the life you want to live.

## Step 5—Tolerate

Challenging and practicing doing something that initially makes you feel uncomfortable may add to your discomfort. That's okay! For Gina, when she started saying no in the small things, she would feel anxious or uncertain. The short-term effects of this change in behavior made her feel uncomfortable. This isn't uncommon. In fact, it's completely natural. Yet, even in her discomfort, Gina chose to keep moving forward. After practicing at home, with friends, and with trusted coworkers, Gina began to feel more comfortable than ever saying no. In addition to practice, here are a few other strategies you can implement to mitigate feeling uncomfortable when saying no.

- Journal
- Meditate
- Talk to a friend
- Reach out to your therapist or leadership coach

As I shared earlier, while your feelings are real and important, they are not necessarily facts. Using any combination of the practices above may help you process the anxiety you can experience when trying to stop people-pleasing. Remember, just because your body might feel like it's in danger doesn't mean it's true! You've got this!

## STEP 6—CELEBRATE

When Gina eventually told Madison, "No," she thought her work world might fall apart. The anxiety bubbling in her stomach always told her to say yes. The inner critic in her mind told her she wasn't secure enough in her position to tell her boss no. Fear controlled her. That is, until she started working through why she felt like she couldn't say no. She was worried that saying no would affect her upcoming performance evaluation. She feared by not being at the event, she would miss out on the opportunity to attend future events. Her inner critic even went as far to catastrophize that her boss would yell at her and say she had to be there regardless of her previous commitment. When Gina finally decided to tell Madison no, she had worked to become as comfortable with the word as she could be. Sure, she felt a little scared, but she knew what she needed to do. Contrary to what Gina assumed, Madison didn't push for her to go to the event. Instead, Madison said, "I understand. I'll ask Harold to go," then walked away. Oftentimes, our mind plays out worst-case scenarios that are not based in reality. Success! Gina chose to live in freedom over fear, choosing herself.

It's important to do what we are scared to do sometimes. And it's equally important to celebrate your wins! This type of brave step is the perfect opportunity to go and grab your brag book. Write down what you did, and why you are proud of yourself. Your wins should be celebrated, big or small. Right now, go grab your brag book and write down one thing you are proud of yourself for doing. Bonus points if it's within the realm of saying no to someone or choosing not to people-please. I'm so proud of you!

# TAKE BACK YOUR VOICE

My own people-pleaser recovery journey took off when I quit my VP job. As much as I wanted to stay for my students, enough was enough. I typed up my letter of resignation, and I created a plan. Over the years, I had watched various colleagues leave. After they had departed, I listened to some of the leadership belittling their name and character. When I planned to leave my position, I knew how I wanted to leave—surrounded by the people I cared about with dignity and respect.

I told my staff and students first in a bittersweet meeting. They encouraged me, and I was able to tell them how much they meant to me. It was what I wanted. When I told my boss the following week, I was able to hand him the papers and leave with dignity. The moment was all mine. I left the way I wanted to. Even though it was scary, I chose to live my life the way I wanted to live it, not in fear but in freedom.

Ironically, lately I've been saying yes more than no, because my life is finally in alignment! When I say, "No," I mean it which makes each "yes" even more possible and meaningful. I wouldn't be currently pursuing my dreams if I had stayed at the college. I had to start saying no to open the doors I wanted to say yes to. I knew I needed to leave my workplace to grow, and maybe you do too. Or maybe you're trying to decide if you should stay in a situation. I can't tell you whether going or staying is inherently right for you, but I can teach you some things about boundaries, getting to know yourself, and psychological safety in the workplace in the following chapters that may help you decide.

# Chapter 3

# THERE IS ONLY ONE YOU

THERE IS NO one exactly like you. There is no one on this planet who can love or lead just like you, or who has your specific experiences. You are a unique and dynamic individual simply because you are you with your lived experiences. In fact, you are a treasure. However, as "one man's trash is another man's treasure," as precious as you are, some people aren't going to see your value for what it truly is. In a harsh truth that took me a long time to accept, some people will get to know you and decide they just do not like you. It hurts, and it can be confusing, especially in our younger years as we are figuring out who we are. In these moments where people do not recognize our value, it can make us feel incredibly vulnerable, rejected, and lead us to asking self-deprecating questions:

- Why did he break up with me?
- Why doesn't she ask me to go have lunch with her anymore?
- Have I done something to hurt them?
- What did I do wrong?
- Is there something wrong with me?

These questions are so natural. There is not a single person on the planet who doesn't want to be loved and accepted. It's human nature 101. Decades of social psychology research show that our deep human need to be liked, loved, and belong drives in-group bias, where we instinctively favor people who feel "like us" while unconsciously devaluing those perceived as part of an "out-group." We have a natural, instinctual desire to belong. So, when we are rejected or ignored, we are often left feeling inadequate, helpless, out of control, or inferior. Is this difficult? Yes. But the truth is this. Not everyone is going to like you. (I know! Why not?! Why can't everyone we like also like us back?) That is what I thought for so long until one very important realization changed me.

One of the best lessons I've ever realized in life is that *I* do not like everyone. So, why did I think that everyone should like me? An interesting truth is that while we all share a desire to be loved and accepted, we receive love and acceptance in different ways. One example is Dr. Gary Chapman's well-known 5 Love Languages.[1] Some people feel most loved by spending quality time with their partner, while others feel loved by verbal affirmation. Personally, I am a fan of a thoughtful gift, which my husband is still working on figuring out. We are all different, and that can cause us to connect easily with some folks and not with others.

Some of us will simply not naturally enjoy how another person shows love, their personality, or how they go about their work, and that is okay. And while it can be uncomfortable to feel rejected by a coworker, that does not mean you are not good enough just the way you are. Just as it is okay to not be liked by everyone, you do not have to like everyone. I often say I am not everyone's cup of tea, but to some people, the ones that matter, I am their favorite glass of champagne.

However, not all challenges to liking someone else are just about these neutral differences in people's personalities or preferences. For example, you don't have to like or spend time with someone who constantly crosses your boundaries. You don't have to fight to stay friends with someone who consistently disrespects your values. Just as another person does not owe you love and acceptance "just because," you don't owe that to others either. A desperate need to be liked by others is not worth sacrificing your self-respect or who you are at your core.

Real talk. Your time, energy, and love are all valuable and limited. You don't have to spend your invaluable traits and resources on people who don't value them too. To quote my dear granny, "Where one won't, ten others will." This was her early relationship advice to tell me that if one man doesn't love you for who you are, there are ten others who will. It was her version of "there are plenty of fish in the sea."

Life is short, and change is inevitable. You deserve to be surrounded by people you love and who love you, exactly the way you are. I wasted too many years and emotions on trying to force relationships that were not a good fit. You know when a relationship (personal or professional) feels like you are shoving your foot in a glass slipper that does not belong to you. Growing your self-confidence and emotional intelligence will bring you closer to knowing who you truly are and, thus, closer to your true people. The people who fit in your life will be like a perfect pair of jeans. It's time to make a choice. Are you going to be your true, authentic, messy self, or are you going to live as a "chameleon," showing only the pretty, perfect, and polished parts you think others want?

## BEING A CHAMELEON

Do you find yourself assessing every situation you are in, then coming up with a game plan, trying to control the outcome or everyone's impressions? Are you changing your language, conversations, clothes, or maybe even beliefs depending on who you're talking to? In short, are you being a chameleon, reacting differently in certain situations, feeling the pressure to be someone else, changing your true colors to fit the situation? This is what it feels like to be a chameleon.

Being a chameleon is the opposite of being confident, because I believe that authenticity and confidence go hand in hand. The chameleon version of us usually shows up out of an internal need for self-preservation. Chameleons learn what another person wants to hear and adapt their language, communication style, or even beliefs depending on who they are currently speaking to. It may not sound bad at first glance, and you can feel like you are just trying to fit in. However, there is a difference between wanting to be liked by a colleague and giving up parts of who you are: politely laughing at their not-so-funny joke, dressing in all black or navy to not stand out in a board meeting, or nodding in agreement when your boss tells you that a woman could never do a particular job (even though you know she could). Being a chameleon is not being you. It is a kind of representation of who you think the other person in the room wants you to be. Eventually, this will lead you to lose your voice, character, confidence, and even yourself. It is unsustainable and robs us of real connection.

While all chameleon behaviors are not exactly same, they do share similar feelings and views about themselves. People who tend to operate as chameleons practice a variety of the following:

- High empathy for others, but not for themselves
- Distrusting themselves or others
- People-pleasing tendencies
- Perfectionism
- Fearful of conflict and rejection
- Difficulty making decisions without affirmation from others
- Consistently filtering their language and actions

I learned how to be a chameleon from my mom. With her many new jobs, new people, and new places, I watched her routinely change to be who she thought she needed to be. So, I learned to change to be who I thought people needed me to be. Moving towns, schools, and homes made this my go to strategy for adapting. As an adult, I continued to take this practice home and to work, and eventually, as it does for all people, it became unsustainable. It led me to feel burned out, voiceless, lonely, and directionless. Then, I found out there is a better way.

Are you being a chameleon in your personal or professional lives? Pause now and ask yourself these questions:

- Do I believe what I am saying?
- Am I being myself?
- What do I want?
- Is this who I am?
- Am I agreeing to just agree?

Being a chameleon may feel like the easiest option when encountering new situations; however, it can cause us to eventually slip into bad habits or negative thought or relationship patterns. For example, chameleons often end up resenting the people they love for not truly knowing them or feeling angry at them for not understanding. Over time, we can wake up feeling unseen and disconnected, wondering how the people closest to us missed who we really are when we never gave them a chance to see us clearly in the first place.

Choosing to learn about yourself and authentically being the amazing person you are is worth it. I promise. It's time to stop shrinking yourself and walk in confidence. The world is missing out on your brilliance if you are hiding behind a mask and others can never get to know the real you. Living an authentic and chosen life is better than living the life of someone you are not. But there is a hard side to this choice.

As much as I truly believe living in the truth of who you are will bring you joy, I also know choosing to be yourself is the more difficult and vulnerable option. Throughout my career, I have worked with women who have experienced short-term benefits from being a chameleon. Let's take Danielle as an example. Danielle has been working for the same company for the last fifteen years. Since working there, she has steadily climbed the ranks. In her twenties she started out as a coordinator, and she is now a revered VP. Her work is great and she has also cultivated friendships with nearly every coworker. She is well liked in the office, highly successful, and, from the outside looking in, has a work life some people may envy. However, Danielle has been operating as a chameleon and is internally miserable, uncertain, and feels alone.

While she is well liked by many people, Danielle admits that her work colleagues and friends don't really know her. When speaking with fellow VPs she sometimes finds herself verbally agreeing with them, but internally she is uncomfortable with what she is agreeing to. When she talks with other coordinators or managers, she finds herself doing the same thing. Her shoulders are tense, her breathing is shallow, and she is almost always on guard. Then, when she comes home, she has little space for life outside of work. She used to love making sweet treats and taking late-night walks with her pup. Now, she comes home exhausted and ready to retreat to her room with whatever easy meal she can carry (and usually a glass of wine to numb her feelings). She is filled with anxiety from overanalyzing each conversation she had earlier in the day and has been steadily walking toward emotional burnout.

One night, Danielle found herself in her kitchen, sobbing. She felt shame for being so sad about the seemingly great life she has, yet she saw no way out. With tears in her eyes, she went to bed, woke up, and headed to work the next day. All these years later, Danielle feels like she has lost her identity, and she started to falter in her ability to function day-to-day. She was passed up for the latest promotion. Some of her colleagues stopped trusting her after comparing what she says to them versus what she says saying to others. After all this effort to please everyone and stay "in" with them, she was now alone, stagnant in her career, and exhausted from the life that seemed to just be happening to her.

As you can see, early on, being a chameleon didn't seem like a bad thing. Danielle thought she was doing what she needed to do to survive at her job. She wanted to be liked and accepted at all costs. In a way, being a chameleon helped her achieve her goal. She got the life she always "wanted," but she sacrificed pieces of herself along the way. Eventually, she lost herself, waking up to the reality of what being a chameleon cost her. *Being liked does not always equate to being respected.* Studies consistently show respect is one of the most desired traits in a relationship (personal and professional).

Admittedly, some days it may feel easier to be a chameleon than to be yourself. It may seem easier to laugh at the joke or agree with your manager than to speak up for what you believe. But, living as a false representative of who you are is not living in confidence. And just like Danielle, eventually it will become unsustainable and expose us as inauthentic and inconsistent. We must take off the chameleon colors and be confident in the person we are, living the truths of who we are, even when it is scary.

And while friends, family, and partners can be valuable encouragers, ultimately it is you who must choose to live in authenticity and confidence. If you wait for someone to hand you confidence, you will be waiting for the rest of your life. You must claim it, and I would suggest claiming it now. Name your inner critic and tell it to take a nap or eat a Snickers. Start the brag book to ground yourself in what you have done. Choose you. The real you.

## WHAT WE SAY WITHOUT SAYING IT

Thus far, our practices have been focused on intentional choices. However, there are also unintentional nonverbal cues which can add or detract to our confidence. A nonverbal cue is something we communicate without saying anything. It's things like the way we stand and how we position ourselves in a room. It may be the lack of eye contact with a supervisor or the choice to sit at the head of the table for a meeting. These behavioral choices communicate something to others about how we view ourselves.

These social cues can not only be nonverbal, but sometimes, they are not even intentional. You might be thinking, "Well, if it's unintentional, how do I stop doing it?" Great question. To change unintentional social cues that may be working against you, you must bring awareness to what you are doing—bringing it into conscious focus. An example of this practice would be mentally walking through your day and remembering how you stood or held yourself in the conversations you had with your coworkers or your partner. You can keep a journal, noting your feelings throughout the day, and identify any triggers, situations, or people who led to a particular unwanted feeling. When we are aware of the unintentionally unconfident actions we are doing, we can replace them with intentionally confident ones. Consider these examples.

| Unintentional Unconfident Actions | Intentional Confident Actions |
| --- | --- |
| Covering your mouth while speaking to a coworker | Putting both of your hands at your side or on your hips |
| Avoiding eye contact with a boss | Choosing to keep eye contact throughout the meeting |
| Leaning against a wall in a crowded room | Inserting yourself with a group of coworkers with whom you would like to be better acquainted |
| Choosing a seat away from the head of the table when you are leading the meeting | It's time to take your seat at the head of the table! Speak clearly to the room with your head up and your shoulders back. |

For a more in depth read on the psychology of nonverbal communication, scan the QR code to access the downloadable PDF bonus chapter.

So, why do we engage in nonverbal and/or unintentional social cues that work against us? Sometimes we unintentionally shrink ourselves because we are either overwhelmed or stuck in our mind not knowing how to act. Events like going to the office Christmas party or meeting your partner's parents can bring anxiety or cause anyone to get stuck in their head because we want to be liked and belong. In these moments, one of the ways you can bring yourself out of a mental spiral or feeling "stuck" is by simply choosing to do another physical action. Go wash your hands in cold water and focus on what the water feels like. Keep some sour candy on you to pop in your mouth. Actions like this can help center your mind and open a window to process the bigger emotions you are feeling later.

In short, replacing the unintentional with the intentional can help you build confidence and bring you closer to living authentically rather than as a chameleon or on autopilot. (And if your friends ask why you're carrying around sour candies, just let them know you are focused on growing into the most confident and sure person you can be.)

## BEING A "GOOD GIRL"

When I was younger, I used to shrink myself by trying to be perfect to everyone, everywhere, all the time. Because growing up, I wanted to be a "good girl." I was the kid in class who always raised her hand, never got up before my teacher told me I could, and offered to read out loud. And I was rewarded for it. My teachers showed me kindness and complimented me. As the perpetually new kid, it felt nice. Their affirmations felt like the kind of belonging I was longing for. And while my family's constant moves and changes taught me to be adaptable, it also reinforced some less than healthy behaviors. For example, I became the one willing to do what needed to be done even if I didn't want to do it. I was ready to put others first, even if it was a detriment to myself. I so desperately wanted to fit in and be accepted that I didn't even know how to recognize my own needs, much less put them first. Again, as a child, this didn't seem like a big deal. My teachers, parents, and friends all liked me. What harm could come from a kid who was just acting to belong and feel loved?

Turns out, those early habits of putting myself aside for belonging followed me after childhood. As an adult woman, I still wanted to be a good girl. The team player who didn't complain and showed up ready to work hard every day. So, I would regularly stay for the late-night meeting. I wouldn't leave early. I would volunteer to work the weekend events that no one else wanted to. Looking back, I let myself be a doormat at times, but I strove to be a pleasant doormat. If my actions were a physical representation of a doormat, in giant letters it would say, "Welcome! Of course I will do that for you!" and it would be impeccably clean. And while it felt nice to be affirmed at points, I began to notice that colleagues, "friends," or partners at the time simply took advantage of my willingness.

On one sunny day, I had done what I rarely did. I took a day off from a toxic jobsite where I had been habitually too accommodating. I was so excited to be home with my girls and spend quality time with the people who mattered the most to me. As I was playing with my oldest, my phone rang. It was work. I had a choice. Do I pick up the phone on my day off or do I let it ring? Of course they knew I was off, because I am the "good" employee who overcommunicates. They approved it, and I had set an out-of-office reply on my calendar. Why were they calling me?

I chose to answer instead of letting it go to voicemail or making them call back if it was a true emergency. Looking back, I can't even remember the conversation because it was so unnecessary. But what I do remember is this not only happened once, but repeatedly. And I eventually realized that it was not about the phone calls, but the intense fear I had: If I didn't answer, what would happen? Would I fall from good graces and be seen as the no-longer-valued employee, always accessible and available? As painful and conflicting as these moments were, they were also educational. I started to ask myself the hard questions. Why did I pick up the phone? Why didn't I stay inside with my kids? Why did I feel pressured to pick up the phone on my day off, while I was riding in the car with my family? Why did I feel the way I felt in the moment? I wasn't thrilled with the answers that came back.

At that point in my life, my self-confidence was low, and I still wanted to be the good girl. I was truly afraid of not being valued or even liked by my boss, coworkers, friends, etc. Being a good girl brought a steadiness and a warped sense of peace. I wanted so badly to be accepted. I was willing to be the good girl even if it meant allowing other people to disrespect my boundaries, time, and myself. What I didn't realize at the time was that what I actually needed to do was stop people-pleasing, trust myself, acknowledge my power, and confidently use my voice. That was something I had to learn and something we will explore together.

## IT'S TIME TO BE FREE

It may seem easier to keep living as a well-liked chameleon, existing within the bounds of who other people think you should be and who they believe you are. But no matter how well you blend in, you are still trapped in a truth that is not your own. It is only when you find the confidence to be yourself that you will experience freedom. Freedom to chase after the dreams you've been quietly holding in your heart. Freedom to speak your mind to your partner. Freedom to be the wonderful parent you are without feeling shame from fellow parents. Freedom to be the uniquely gifted, talented, and courageous person you have always been. The time is now to start living without fear holding you back. Time to be confident in yourself and move toward what you know you can do.

Chapter 4:

# THE IMPORTANCE OF EMOTIONAL INTELLIGENCE

## WHAT IS EMOTIONAL INTELLIGENCE?

ONE OF THE great benefits of working on your self-confidence is that, inevitably, you will also work on growing your emotional intelligence. Emotional intelligence is one's ability to understand your emotions and the emotions of others around you. So, why is it important to be emotionally intelligent, aware of my emotions and those of others? Because, at the end of the day, feelings are important information, but we often understand them as less important than our thoughts and, due to their discomfort or intensity, can even fear them. I have had so many clients or colleagues tell me they hate feeling their feelings, or express discomfort when becoming "emotional," crying, etc. These emotions that we so often try to avoid are actually important sources of information that are essential to understand.

In graduate school while training to be a therapist, I remember my supervisor telling me that when someone is crying in a session, you do NOT offer them a tissue; instead just keep them visibly accessible. At first, I thought this advice was rude and killed my southern polite upbringing. She then explained that when we do this, we are signaling to the other person we are uncomfortable with their emotions. She suggested it is the nonverbal equivalent of "Here is a tissue to wipe up your tears, and please stop emoting." Thankfully, at this point in my life and career, I now see the beauty in emotions. (Yes, even crying is a beautiful experience, even if you might be like me an "ugly crier.") In short, emotional intelligence is one of the essential keys to our success and meaningful connections with self and others.

Another important note on our wide range of emotions. As humans, we cannot selectively choose which emotions to "mute." For example, when you numb sadness, you also diminish your ability to experience joy. The practice of numbing difficult emotions tends to also reduce the ones we enjoy feeling. When we try to silence a part of ourselves as important as our emotional experience, we hinder ourselves from knowing more about ourselves and the world around us. To grow your emotional intelligence, you must feel your feelings from a position of curiosity, rather than avoidance or self-judgment. You must also be willing to open your ears, eyes, and heart to sit with others' emotions. For some of you, this may sound easy, but living this out, as a woman, might also sound scary or intimidating.

From what seems like the dawn of time, women have been told by bosses, coworkers, partners, and anyone in between, how their emotions are a problem. And they have certainly not been welcome in leadership or professional settings. A woman can go to college, and raise kids if she chooses, but many people still struggle to believe that she could lead a team at work, not with all those emotions (insert eye roll). It is ironic to consider that culture reveres a woman's ability to teach ethics and morals to the next generation, but their emotions are "too much" for the workplace. To be frank, it doesn't make sense, and it's beyond frustrating. Of course, having emotions is not a gendered experience. All of us—no matter who we are, what gender we are, how old we are, what we look like—have complex, beautiful, difficult, painful, and joyful emotions. It's called being human. And while emotions have been labeled upon women as a hindrance, the truth is emotions are a necessary part of the human experience, *and therefore essential to leadership.* I would also argue, and research supports this notion, that as women, emotional intelligence can be one of our greatest superpowers.

In my experience as a leader, especially as the sole female C-suite leader at the time, I felt different than my male counterparts regarding how I led because I led with both my head and my heart. This looked like taking the time to get to know my staff, their family stories, hopes, dreams, and fears. I was astutely attuned to the emotions of those I worked with when they walked in the door, participated in meetings, or were given a directive. Yes, tapping into emotional information takes more time as a leader, but I promise it also pays exponential dividends. Observing a coworker's body language, facial reactions, verbal response, choice of words, or tone often told me so much more about how they were feeling and potentially thinking than the words they spoke. If we pay attention, people can become quite obvious and have many telltale signs about their emotions. When we open our eyes, listen, care, and pay attention to these cues with curiosity and not judgment, our leadership takes on an angle of compassion, and the world becomes a little less complicated.

## WE CAN'T IGNORE OUR FEELINGS

One of my favorite ways I've ever heard emotions described is that they are like driving in a car with children. We don't let children drive the car, but we also don't lock them in the trunk! They are co-passengers on the journey. It's a similar situation for your emotions. If you are feeling an emotion, stuffing it in the trunk of your mind won't magically fix your situation. The emotion is still there, begging (maybe screaming!) to be heard, no matter how far back you stuff it. Instead of shoving them in the trunk or to the back of the metaphorical closet, you can instead allow yourself to experience it, feel it, name it, and process it. It is important to note that just because you have an emotion doesn't mean it has to control you. This is often one of our greatest fears with emotions, that they are somehow going to take over. Yes, your emotions are real and deserve your attention, but that does not mean they are always true to the situation. Instead, they are information to pay attention to, be curious about, and ask questions of.

For example, if you feel fearful about presenting at the all-staff meeting at the end of the week, that is not unnatural. Public speaking is often cited as the number one feared activity (which is why it is one of my favorite things to coach women on). However, experiencing fear about the meeting doesn't mean it will go poorly or that you suck at your job. It is just a feeling, and it doesn't have to control you or the experience. But if you ignore it or try to stuff it down, it is far more likely to control you and negatively impact your behavior in the meeting. Emotions can be quite stubborn and demand to be heard. It benefits us to learn how to acknowledge and process them.

You might even be thinking to yourself, "Kasi, I know I need to feel my feelings, but they are so overwhelming and at times confusing. Honestly, I don't even know what exactly I'm feeling, and I am scared of what others will think if I show my emotions. All I do know is I don't feel confident even knowing where to start." This is a very common reaction for someone who is newly attempting to get familiar interacting with their feelings. At this time, we ask important questions like, "What do we do with what we feel?" "How do we identify what we are feeling?" "How do understand a feeling without letting it take over?" Thankfully, you have already practiced this skill earlier in the book. Just like with your inner critic, the very first way we begin have a healthy relationship with our emotions is "name it to know it."

## WHAT IF I DON'T KNOW WHAT I'M FEELING?

As we've discussed, some emotions are harder to identify than others. Let's take another look at Danielle from chapter two. While living as a chameleon, she found herself crying in her kitchen at least once a week. Obviously, she could deduce she was sad. The tears and hopeless feeling in her stomach offered obvious indicators that she was not okay, but she was not sure what this meant or what to do with these feelings. The sadness was so overwhelming and contradictory to the life she was living that she was unable to process why she was feeling the way she was. If Danielle was in front of me right now (or it were you with an uncertain emotional experience), I would tell her the following: "You're not crazy. You are human, and, yes, emotions can feel hard. But they are a part of our experience, and I am here for you." Then I would introduce her to the following tactics to help her name and process through what she is feeling.

## Name the Feeling

Have you heard about the feelings wheel (see below)[2]? It is an illustration breaking down our more commonly identified core emotions into more precise language. This can help you identify and start to process emotions that are harder to name or understand because it gives you language and a visual map of how to expand basic emotions. Sadly, we are not always taught about emotions beyond general descriptions of sad, mad, or happy. As humans, our emotions are far more complex than that. Using the feelings wheel provides a method for communicating the complexities of our emotional experiences, beyond the surface. For example, Danielle knew she was feeling sad when she was crying. But if she looked at the feelings wheel, she would have noticed words that allowed her to better name what she was feeling such as isolated, inferior, empty, and disappointed in the inauthentic life she was living. You don't need a degree to use the feelings wheel. You can take a picture of the feelings wheel in this book, do a simple Google search, and print one off, or there are even pillows online with the feelings wheel you can purchase! On a fun note, I would recommend this diagram as well as the movies *Inside Out* and *Inside Out 2* as great tools for children, parents, and adults who want to better understand their emotions and increase their emotional intelligence. Having tools like this can come in handy to be able to accurately identify what you are feeling in the moment.

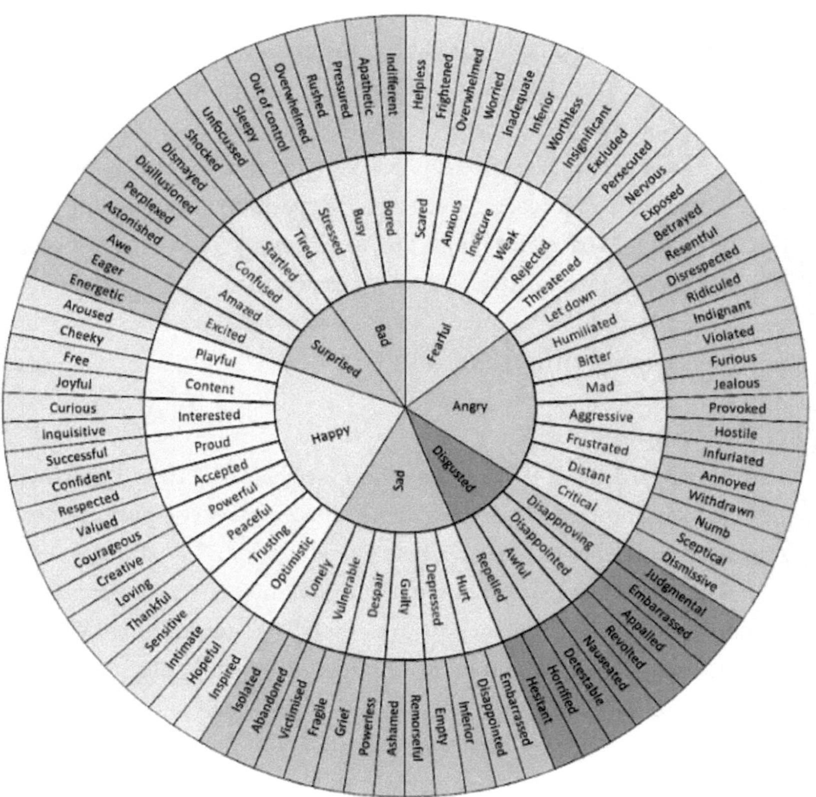

## START JOURNALING OR EXPAND YOUR BRAG BOOK

In chapter one, we discussed starting a brag book to encourage confidence. This strategy can also be used as a tool to increase emotional intelligence by tracking your emotional experiences throughout the day. When you practice accurately identifying a positive or negative trigger, note it in your brag book or separate journal if you prefer. Write down what you were doing, who you were with, and how it made you feel. When you get upset with your partner for leaving their underwear on the floor for the hundredth time or being interrupted by a colleague yet again in the meeting, you can note it in your journal making sure to include the all the names of the emotions you experienced at that time.

While your brag book is important for a variety reasons, if you choose to keep a separate journal, it can serve as a place for all your feelings and thoughts. A journal is meant to be a safe place where you can share what you loved, hated, or wished went differently during the day or even the last hour. You can detail your wins in your journal as well as use it as a space to record what you feel like you can't say out loud, like what you wish you could really say to your boss, using all the colorful and explicit words you choose. A journal is where you can share how you feel about your love life or desire for it. And it will listen without shame, guilt, or reprehension. You can just dump everything you're thinking and feeling onto paper (or a digital journal on a computer if preferred). When we share what we're feeling, we create space in our minds to process it. Journaling allows us to create the space to move forward in these difficult emotional experiences.

Additionally, I want to offer you some freedom from any rigidity with this practice. On some days you may only write two sentences, while on others you may write two pages. There is no right or wrong way to journal. There is simply doing it. Journal to learn more about yourself and what you are feeling. Do it to note what positive and negative triggers you experienced throughout your day. Similar to a brag book, your journal is a kind of mirror. Yet unlike your brag book, this mirror sees all of you. It shows the beauty marks, but also leaves room to acknowledge the scars. A journal can be a safe space to share your successes like a new promotion and to process through the more difficult emotions like fear of losing someone you love. Both "mirrors" are tools to help you grow your emotional intelligence.

## GIVE YOURSELF A CONTAINER TO FEEL IT ALL

No one minds experiencing happy feelings. No one loses sleep over having an easygoing, confident, joyful, grateful life (except those who fear losing it all). However, fear, stress, contempt, and anger—just to name a few—can make life feel like an uncomfortable experience from the time you take your head off your pillow to the time you lay it back down. As it is with children, just because you tell emotions to be quiet, doesn't mean they will. Sometimes, it makes them cry even louder. But why do children cry? It's because they are trying to communicate something. Emotions are the same way. They are trying to tell you something about yourself. When you try to stuff down your emotions, they do not just go away. They are still there, and like children, they tend to get louder if you do not listen.

However, unlike the urgency of children, this is where we have a choice about the execution of the "when" and "how" we listen to our emotions.

We don't have to internalize every emotion exactly when we feel it. We can wait. Maybe you're at work, and there isn't a safe place for you to cry. Maybe you're at a friend's birthday party, and you don't want to make a scene. You have control over what you do with your emotions, and it's okay to wait to process what you are feeling until you are in a safe situation to do so. This is not the same as ignoring or "stuffing" your feelings. This is a choice made to delay due to the social constructs you are facing. Just remember, if you do choose to wait, the emotions will come back until you name and acknowledge them. We can process pain, joy, and every other feeling when we're ready but try not to selectively choose to feel only positive emotions. Remember, if we numb pain, we also numb joy. You get to decide when, but not if, processing your emotions is best for you.

Whenever you've determined that you are ready to feel your feelings, you can also offer yourself a "container." Practically, this looks like possibly setting a time for fifteen minutes to just feel it all. You can cry it out, journal, or do whatever you need to do in the time you gave yourself to just feel. Giving yourself a container can help you process your emotions while not getting lost in them. Having a container of time can help you feel in control, not your emotions. It helps affirm your control and agency.

## Don't Just Take My Word for It

As much as I appreciate you reading what I have to share, it's important to know that there are many incredible people who have spoken extensively on these same subjects. Over the past several decades, many great psychologists and coaches have shared their insights on emotional intelligence. How amazing is it that we live in a time where we can learn so much about what is going on in our minds? And, while I won't recommend every book on the subject, I will highly recommend two. *Daring Greatly*[3] by Brene Brown and *Emotional Intelligence: Why it can matter more than IQ*[4] by Daniel Goleman. Both books are great resources which specifically address emotional intelligence and the vulnerability of feeling and sharing emotions with others. Brene Brown is the queen of vulnerability and connection, and one of the most important social scientists of our time. I highly recommend any and all of her books, talks, articles, on the subject matter.

## Reach Out to a Therapist or a Leadership Coach

While journaling, learning, and reading about emotional intelligence can help guide your emotional intelligence journey, it can also be helpful to speak directly with someone who has studied the subject. There is no shame or judgment in asking for more direct, personal help. We have more resources available to us than our grandmothers or even our mothers had, so I implore you to use them. In my own journey I sought out coaches, therapists, mentors, and friends as I attempted to process the complicated emotions I felt when leaving my job at the college.

For any emotionally intense experience, particularly trauma, I highly encourage seeking external help in processing emotions as it can be overwhelming. Trauma-informed therapists have some unique skills sets, understanding, and even training like EMDR (Eye Movement Desensitization and Reprocessing) that is specifically designed to work with your brain's design. You will benefit from an experienced professional guiding you through this process. They are skilled at creating a safe container to help you process emotions that may feel too difficult or overwhelming.

Once I finally reached out to a therapist, I had pushed down feelings of being worthless, dejected, rejected, and more for years. I needed to talk to someone. Yes, I had incredible family and friends who were willing to listen, but there is a unique power in having an outside person who can be objective while you freely express your thoughts and emotions. I needed a space to verbally process with a person I could trust outside of my everyday life.

Perhaps today, you find yourself in a position similar to mine. After years of pushing down your feelings, you need to talk to someone to help kickstart the process of healing, emotional awareness, and increased emotional intelligence. I recommend reaching out to a therapist or a leadership coach who is well-versed in teaching and encouraging emotional expression and intelligence. It is important to also look for a therapist or coach who is licensed, credentialed, and trustworthy. You may be spending a significant amount of your time (and/or money) with this person, so take your time to find the right person. Try out a couple of different people if necessary, ask trusted friends for referrals, browse the internet/reviews, but take action. Find the best fit for you, your current needs, and goals.

## CHANGE IS INEVITABLE AND SOMETIMES UNPREDICTABLE

Life is full of predictable changes like making the choice to accept a new job and unpredictable changes like how your boss will react to a mistake. In full transparency, when you start growing in emotional intelligence, every relationship in your life will change in some way. You might be thinking, "I hope so! I need my life to change! I don't want to keep living this way!" And while I hope that all your changes are positive, it is important to recognize change in any capacity causes a chain reaction. When you change the way you act, it impacts multiple areas of your life. Some effects you will welcome while others may surprise or even disappoint you. There are good changes that may come from your different approach to the world like buying a new car or the dream house you have always wanted. There are also difficult changes like being laid off out of the blue or significant changes to an important relationship. When we are different, the world (and people) around us react differently as well.

Additionally, while we can always count on change, we can't always count on how we will react to those changes. This is an important part of growing in emotional intelligence. Part of this journey is becoming more comfortable examining which emotions arise from the unexpected. You can't predict exactly how you will feel when your boss gives you the promotion you've been working toward, or when the doctor calls to tell you about the results from the test last week. Sometimes even "good news," like getting a promotion, can elicit unexpected negative emotions, like the fear of "now I have to prove myself."

Of course, we can't prepare exactly for every single situation we will experience in this life. I know I tried for many years, and catastrophizing was my go-to emotional response that robbed me of joy. I needed new ways to process and understand my reactions. In order to do this, we can learn more about ourselves, process how we feel about situations more accurately, and also conjure a little trust that things generally work out over time when we use our resources wisely.

Go ahead and grab a sheet of paper and something to write with. Write down a situation that has been on your mind the most this past week or month. Maybe it was a meeting with your boss or a conversation with a family member. Maybe it was an interaction with a friend or a potential opportunity. With that in mind, answer the questions below about your situation.

- Why is this situation sticking with me?

- How do I feel about this situation?
- What do I want to happen with this situation?
- Do I want to feel my feelings, or do I have an urge to put them in a dark corner and never let them see the light of day?

Feel free to take your time answering the questions above. There's no rush.

If you are having trouble, remember, certain feelings are easier to identify than others. For example, if someone cuts you off when you're driving or cuts in line at the grocery store, it can make you feel disrespected or annoyed. If someone chooses to pay for your meal, it can make you feel grateful and appreciated. In these moments, identifying what you feel and processing them doesn't seem like an overwhelming task. But not all situations are so cut and dry, so I encourage you to take a moment, slow down, and examine, name, and process your feelings. If needed, go back to the feelings wheel and search for more specific words to identify what you are experiencing.

Let's take another look back at Danielle. She had achieved her dreams. The big office, the loving friendships, the luxury apartment. Yet even with so many goals achieved, she was miserable. Why did she feel so sad when she had so much of what she thought she wanted? What exactly was she feeling? What triggered her emotional breakdown? It doesn't always seem obvious at first, and it's not always just one feeling. Feelings have a way of sharing space, particularly in complex situations, and that can lead to complicated, coexisting, or even competing feelings.

Complicated situations are a breeding ground for these types of emotions. It can be frustrating or disappointing to experience moments like Danielle's where the pain we feel inside seems to contradict the life we are living. It's crying at the kitchen table after receiving an award for excellent service at work. It's complicated, disappointing, and shameful feelings that seem to appear out of nowhere. When the cause is not obvious or the emotions and situation don't seem to "match," identifying what we are feeling and processing our feelings is not an easy task.

For Danielle, part of the reason her emotional experience was complicated was because the root of her sorrow wasn't one specific problem. Instead, it was years of making inauthentic choices meant to preserve her happiness, which led her in the complete opposite direction. She made one decision after another contrary to what she really wanted, triggering complicated emotions, which then triggered another complicated emotion, and another complicated emotion, until it felt like her world was spinning with no sense of control.

If you've ever experienced something like Danielle, let me assure you, you are not alone. Many of us make decisions that seem like the smart choice or good idea, only later to figure out it was inauthentic to who we really are. Yet, even if you have done this again and again for years, you do not have to be stuck in a perpetual cycle of emotional turmoil and triggers. Anyone can begin their growth toward emotional intelligence today. While it is not always an easy journey, often initially spurring anxious cycles of self-doubt and a fear of failure, it ultimately is freeing to learn new ways to process through emotions and build self-trust.

As you grow in emotional intelligence, you will be able to set healthier boundaries to protect and cherish the people you love. You will be able to identify the choices that can help you live a more authentic, confident, and free life. In a way, learning about your emotions and how to process not unlike gaining confidence in any other skill. It doesn't just happen. It is something you must actively work on and toward.

## A "ME" SEARCH ON YOURSELF

When I was in the final years of my PhD program, I had to decide on a dissertation topic (which can be as challenging as naming your child … so much pressure to pick the right one!). However, in the early years of this process, when I was just applying to graduate school, I simply had to choose an advisor and particular area of research. I was incredibly grateful to find Dr. Susan Hendrick, as she and her husband were psychologists who studied relationships. Even back then, in addition to my fascination about relationships, I also loved reading about and researching emotional intelligence. As I reflect, I recognize now that these interests were directly related to difficult childhood experiences (parents and siblings, their multiple marriages, and not feeling emotionally validated). In my work with Dr. Hendrick, through psychology and research, I found the validation and explanations that I did not always receive growing up (hence the title of this section, a "me search"). And through the process of healing, I also learned and now truly believe my parents did their best with what they knew.

In addition to my personal experiences that influenced me to learn more about emotional intelligence, as a woman I was also interested in learning about why emotions were taught as a hindrance to my gender. Even from a very early age, I remember people being uncomfortable with my emotions and being told, "You're too much."

Have you been told that before? What does that statement even mean? I know what I absorbed it to mean. You're too much = Don't be too much. But what is too much? How can feeling or expressing an emotion be too much? Also, how can I control how I feel? Can I control how I feel? These were all questions I asked myself for a long time. The message I received was that emotions are bad, and if I express them, that makes people uncomfortable, which, for me, equated to not being liked or accepted. And again, as humans we naturally want to be liked and accepted as our brains equate this to belonging, safety, and ultimately survival.

While graduate school taught me the facts, definitions, and research findings I needed to know about emotional intelligence, I also found myself starting to try to live out what I was learning in the workplace and in relationships. And while I loved going to school for my PhD and I treasure all I learned, I want to be clear that you do not have to get a doctorate in psychology to learn what you need to be an emotionally intelligent person. My goal right here in this book is to give you the tools to leverage emotional intelligence in your workplace, leadership, and/or relationships, saving you from some of the headache and heartache I experienced.

To begin understanding more accurately what you are feeling, you must get to know yourself. As mentioned, you can start by doing a "me" search on yourself. As basic as these questions may sound, you will want to start by asking yourself simple questions like the below:

- What is my favorite color or food and why?
- Do I have a favorite article or type of clothing? What is it and why?
- What is my favorite movie?
- What do I like to read and why?

You may be surprised to realize that you, or others like you, have performed for others for so long that they have truly become unacquainted with their most basic preferences.

After you feel comfortable and confident answering simple questions, you can graduate to questions that may evoke a more emotional response.

- What are my favorite and least favorite childhood memories?
- Do I like the way my parents interact(ed) with me?
- Am I enjoying the life I am currently living?
- Do I like who I have become?
- What do I believe is right and are my actions affirming my beliefs?

This process of learning more about who you are may seem scary or overwhelming, but honoring who you are and what you feel is essential to growing your emotional intelligence. You are a wonder, and what you feel matters. In full transparency, getting to know and love myself (including my emotions) has been a long journey that I would happily do over and again (yes, even the hard parts). Becoming more emotionally intelligent has allowed the relationships in my life to flourish and has been instrumental in creating my life as I know it. Today, after a great deal of work, I can confidently say I'm honoring who I'm meant to be. And I love it.

## THIS IS ONLY THE BEGINNING

It's been over fifteen years since I graduated with my PhD in Psychology, and yet, I'm still learning about emotional intelligence. Yes, I wrote the papers, took the tests, and learned what I needed to be able to best support my clients and team. However, emotional intelligence is not just a set of facts and practices meant for your profession. It's a deeply personal experience that can impact every space of your life.

It is important to realize that by learning about emotional intelligence, you often crack open doors to difficult personal experiences that come with complicated emotions as well as powerful positive realizations. It is a beautiful and challenging journey you'll be walking throughout the rest of your life. It will continue to open your eyes to new perspectives, theories, and practices which can better assist you to achieve the life you want to live personally and professionally. The work can be hard, but I can guarantee you it is more than worth it. In growing your emotional intelligence, you will better know yourself and be able to better recognize and set the boundaries necessary to protect the life you want to live.

# Chapter 5

# SETTING BOUNDARIES IS NECESSARY COMMUNICATION

**W**OMEN CAN DO it all. It's a simple sentence with a complicated message. Of course, it sounds encouraging at first. Yes! I can do it all! Believing you can be there for your family, career, and yourself isn't a bad thing. However, believing you can show up for your friends, family, and job every day meeting all their needs perfectly is completely unrealistic. We must have a frank conversation about what "all" really means.

During my tenure as VP at the college, my little mini-me daughters were just that: little. Thus, they had lots of needs. They needed someone to make their bottles, put a Band-Aid on their non-existent injuries, plan their birthday parties, read "The Kiss Kiss Fish" for the one hundredth time, and do my best to keep them happy and healthy. And I wanted nothing more than to fulfill every need they had. As their mom I'd do anything for my girls. (Note: I'm also grateful for my husband who also helped me do all these things, but moms and dads often feel different pressures.)

For those of you reading this without children, I know there are likely other responsibilities in your life that you would do anything for. Maybe it's taking care of an aging parent, looking after a pet, or managing a team of people at work. We all have people in our lives who count on us, and we don't want to let them down. However, we are human, and that means we have limits. No one carries just one responsibility; we have personal, professional, and other needs. Therefore, at times, "having it all" gets complicated.

While working as VP, from the moment I walked into work (sometimes even before) to the moment I got back in the car to go home, I was constantly in meetings, talking, surrounded by people, answering questions, and putting out fires. Don't get me wrong: I'm an extrovert and love people. I loved solving problems and the work I was doing. I saw the team, student, and faculty needs, and I wanted to fulfill them. I wanted to help, make their lives easier, and use my talents well. However, I also had limits and needed boundaries (even though this has always been a hard pill for me to swallow). But I didn't know how to set the boundaries I needed and how to say no. In the past when I set boundaries, I was consumed by guilt. So, I developed a habit of just not setting them. Instead, I continued to say yes far too often, becoming a welcoming, positive, agreeable doormat. Upon reflection, I think, deep down, I didn't feel worthy of having boundaries or protecting my peace. Saying no simply didn't feel like an option.

This took a toll.

After being surrounded by people all day, I was drained and depleted. I felt like I needed a moment of quiet and to not be responsible for another decision. But I didn't just have a responsibility to my team at work, I also had a responsibility to my family. When I would get home the first question my husband would often ask was, "What's for dinner?"—y'all I don't cook, much to my mom's chagrin. It's a seemingly harmless question, yet oftentimes this would be the tipping point of my stress. I was exhausted from the day, and all I wanted was fifteen minutes where someone didn't ask me to make a decision or tug on my arm for a snack. I desperately needed some "not being needed" time.

And even though I could sense what I needed, I felt guilty. I felt guilty for needing a moment, since I had been away from them all day. I love my family. Naturally, I wanted to give them everything they asked for and be the most amazing, happy, present wife and mom. However, like so many of you, I felt I had nothing left to give. It wasn't their fault, so, often, I would place the blame on myself for not having or being enough. Later, my stress compounded upon itself as the toxicity of my workplace increased. I struggled even more to find time to reset or set boundaries. So, I didn't. I kept trying to be everything for everyone, at the expense of myself.

Since I didn't set boundaries in my work or with my family, I fast tracked myself directly into burnout. It felt like I was playing an internal game of tug-o-war, and I was losing. And, perhaps most importantly, the lack of boundaries didn't actually give me more energy, fill my cup, or make me a better mom. Instead, it did the opposite. I had subscribed to this unintentional belief that I could "do it all . . . be it all . . . with perfection and grace." I took on the identity of a martyr, devoting myself to my family, work, and others.

To be fair, they didn't ask me to do this. Early in my childhood, I'd internalized the belief that self-abandonment was the best and only way to survive. It's like I developed this idea that there was a finite amount of care I could give, and if there wasn't enough left over for myself, that was what should be sacrificed. Because of these long-ingrained thought patterns, initially I was terrified to set boundaries. But as I grew in my emotional intelligence, I learned that without boundaries, I couldn't show up as my best self for my team, my family, friends, or myself. And all of those people deserved the healthiest version of me.

You might be wondering what made me afraid to set boundaries. It's a good question and one many of us end up needing to answer. While I was growing up, the idea of setting boundaries, saying no, and prioritizing myself were foreign concepts. I grew up watching my mother, who single-parented my brother and I, lack boundaries and self-sacrifice. Additionally, I believe that at times this led me to assume the other-parent role at an early age, taking care of my brother rather than focusing on myself.

Due to my childhood, my fear of setting boundaries is rooted in my fear of rejection and abandonment. These same fears followed me later in my own family, with my husband and daughters. Then in my professional world, I became a leader who was constantly on high alert, which translated into a mom who was always stressed out, a wife who had a short fuse, and a shell of a woman. I needed boundaries to be able to be my freest and best self, but I didn't know how to set them, and I certainly didn't feel brave enough to try.

## WHAT EXACTLY ARE BOUNDARIES?

It may sounds like an oxymoron, but boundaries are actually what set us free. And yet, boundaries tend to have a bad reputation. As a child and later as an adult, I felt "bad" for wanting to set boundaries with my family, friends, and coworkers because it felt like I was not being there for others as I was taught. Even though I knew what my mind and body needed, my feelings were not on the same page.

It helped me immensely when I realized that boundaries are just another form of communication. They are simply rules we set to help others know how to treat us. For example, when I didn't communicate my needs to my family, they didn't know how I was feeling while they were trying to show me love. When I got home, they simply wanted to connect. By choosing to be uncommunicative about my needs, my family was left believing everything was fine and that I also, was ready to connect when in reality, I wasn't. I was exhausted and operating on a broken system that needed to recharge. Realizing all this helped me know what needed to change in my life, but I didn't want to hurt the people I loved the most by doing so.

The reality of setting boundaries is they inevitably bring change. As mentioned earlier, change can be difficult, even changes meant to better your life. As a leadership coach and keynote speaker, I have spoken with countless individuals who struggle with setting boundaries for this very same reason. They have the same worries I had all those years ago. They fear that if they set boundaries, others will be upset with them. Worse, if they say no at work, there will be negative professional consequences. In speaking with them over the years, I found three kinds of boundaries particularly difficult to set—time, workplace, and emotional boundaries. And specifically for women, I have seen emotional boundaries be the most difficult to establish.

| Time Boundaries | Workplace Boundaries | Emotional Boundaries |
| --- | --- | --- |
| Telling a friend you can only talk to them for thirty minutes on the phone. | Telling your coworker you can't grab a mid-afternoon coffee with them this week because you need to work. | Saying "no" to discussing a topic with a certain person. |
| Setting a timer on your phone to turn off social media apps after a certain amount of time. | Turning your work phone on "do not disturb" at the end of the workday. | Telling a friend, "I don't feel comfortable with how this action is making me feel." |
| Choosing to lock your phone an hour before bedtime. | Leaving the office and walking away from the computer when it's time to go home. | Choosing to no longer be friends with someone who continuously offends you or takes more than gives. |

Again, as women, we are conditioned to be socially aware of others' emotions. Since women have been raised to be conscious and courteous of others' emotions, it makes sense that it can be difficult for women to set boundaries that may affect someone else's emotions. If you have been taught to prioritize others' emotions, why wouldn't you do just that? However, the truth is that emotional boundaries are an important, healthy part of a relationship. If you tell a friend, "No, I can't be there for you in that way," you can still be a good friend. Saying "no" to one thing simply opens the door to say "yes" to something else.

## ONE BOUNDARY = MULTIPLE STEPS

Often, setting a boundary is like trying to hit a moving target. You don't always hit a bull's-eye on the first try. Let's consider the example of Lindsey. For the last two years, Lindsey has worked in a demanding and fast-paced environment. In her role, she has had to meet the needs of various clients, while also encouraging her teammates' goals. It helps that Lindsey is friends with many of her coworkers. She feels comfortable going out to lunch with them as well as asking them for help. The one downside of these relationships is her coworkers like to come and talk with her in her office. As much as she enjoys their company, she finds herself feeling anxious about completing her work, as well as feeling mentally and emotionally depleted. She needs to set a boundary with them, but where should she start? While this is a nuanced example, it is similar to what I see women face on a larger scale. We don't want our coworkers to stop talking to us all together, but we can't keep working in this overwhelmed, distracted way.

She can...

- *Option A*—Close her office door to signal she isn't available to casually catch up at the moment.
- *Option B*—Tell her coworker she can only talk to them for fifteen minutes.
- *Option C*—Set her calendar to "unavailable" until she has completed the necessary work.

None of these options are guaranteed to be the "right" one, and each boundary will elicit a different result. Maybe Lindsey will hit her desired target with the first boundary she sets, and maybe she won't. And, even if her coworkers do receive the message and honor it initially, most boundaries must be reinforced and recommunicated over time. Remember, setting a boundary at first may feel scary, but we must choose the long-term benefits of a boundary over the short-term social comfort of the lack of one. How do you do that? By mastering the -ATES: eliminate, automate, delegate, negotiate, and appreciate.

## 1. ELiminATE WHAT DRAINS YOU

Identifying what activities, habits, or choices drain energy from your life is the start to setting healthy boundaries. However, when in the thick of burnout, it can be difficult to decipher what is draining and what you enjoy. To help, answer the following questions.

- Are there meetings or events I'm going to that no longer serve a purpose?
- Am I surrounded by energy vampires who leave me feeling depleted?
- Which responsibilities or commitments have been making my days more difficult?

Even though it would offer relief, sometimes it can be difficult to say no to something that drains you. When work would ask me to be present for a late-night event with the students, I was initially conflicted. I loved my students and my job, and I wanted to be as present as I possibly could be for them. On the other hand, saying no to a late-night event with my students meant I could say yes to tucking my girls into bed and reading them their favorite bedtime stories. By saying no to an option that felt important but secondary, I opened the option to say yes to the one that mattered most. Being with my daughters.

## 2. Automate What Repeats

Taking even thirty minutes a week to automate your life can free yourself from some of the more routine and depleting activities that eat away at your time. This is a huge time and energy saver! Consider the places in your life where you repeat time-consuming behaviors and automate them.

| For the Workplace | For the Home |
|---|---|
| Create a generic template for the emails you end up sending on a daily or weekly basis. | Schedule the reminder texts you send to your partner about important events in advance. |
| Turn your routine onboarding steps into an accessible checklist you can share with your coworkers. | Create a generic grocery list of items you frequently buy and keep it in your notes app. |
| Create a base form which you can modify for any surveys you send out. | If you tend to order the same meals to go, save the orders in your phone for ease in the future. |
| Build out formulas or macros for any recurring reports. | At the beginning of the month, prepare any celebratory texts to automatically send. |

Just like we charge our phones in advance, it is helpful to create systems that will recharge us so we are not scrambling at the last minute. Remember burnout doesn't always result from life-altering situations. Even the little actions we do add up, and anything you can do to free yourself from some of those little time or energy-consuming actions is worth it. With the growth of artificial intelligence and technology in general, there are many accessible automation options out there to explore. Pause now and take a moment to ask yourself, "What can I automate in my home or work life?"

## 3. Delegate What Can Be Shared

While I work full-time, I am also a full-time mom of the two most amazing little girls. There is no shortage of tasks that need to be done during the day. Sure, I could try doing it all. I could try to wake up at 5 a.m. every day, do my preferred workout, get ready, pack the kids' lunches, make breakfast for the family, drive the kids to school, go straight to my meetings, and so on. Yes, I *could* do it, but I would be miserable. Not only because it is too much for any one human to reasonably take on each day, but also, and unapologetically, I am not and nor shall I ever be a morning person!

As much as the allure of self-sufficiency tries to trick me, I must remember that taking care of everything and everyone every day would not make me feel better. That level of over-commitment always has come at the price of self-abandonment. Burnout would eventually catch up to me sooner rather than later. I would have a blow up, then subsequently breakdown. I would be miserable, and my kids and work would suffer. And now that I've ridden this merry-go-round more than a few times, I delegate. My husband and I work together to split responsibilities so both of us can pursue our careers while being the best parents we can be. Sometimes this looks like a 50/50 split, and sometimes it is more like 60/40 or 70/30 in either his direction or my own. Because rarely is one season of life just like the other, we regularly evaluate how we are sharing the load and adjust with the ebbs and flows. It took a long time to learn this, with more than a little trial and error, but it is such a helpful practice for us now.

To go back to those early days, when my first daughter was born, I struggled to believe I could be a "good" mom and let others help me. For many of her initial birthdays, I would feel an internal pressure to make them magical, Pinterest-worthy, and unforgettable (knowing full well that she was too young to even form life-long memories).

I would plan elaborate themes, shop for the perfect cake, find hyper-specific decorations, arrange intricate party favors, and create themed invitations. All the while, I would stress over all that needed to be done and freak out over the cleanliness of our home. I would become a mom-zilla who repeatedly snapped at her husband and started arguments just to start them. I was the kind of mom I didn't want to be. The worst part was during the party itself; I would be so exhausted that I was unable to be fully with my daughter. Sometime after her second birthday, I finally realized I needed to change my expectations. Even more so, I needed to learn how to delegate and trust the people in my life to do what I didn't have the mental space to do. As small and silly as it may sound, I started with trusting my husband to pick up the cupcakes. Forgoing the one time he brought home Teenage Mutant Ninja Turtle cupcakes to my daughter's princess-themed birthday party, it has been a great success. More importantly, the kids didn't care. And most importantly, I was able to be fully present with my daughter on her special day. I am now beyond grateful for our amazing friends and family who help us, as it really does take a village to raise kids.

At this point, you may be considering what areas of your life you may be able to relinquish some control and/or delegate. I know it can be difficult to have a conversation reassessing responsibilities with a partner or even a coworker. Yes, change is difficult, but you can't keep living in a cycle of burnout, blow up, and breakdown. You (and the people you care for!) deserve boundaries that will protect your time, energy, and peace. Next time you find yourself drained by an overwhelming number of tasks or from your boundaries being pushed, take a moment to ask yourself the following:

- Are there any interns or team members who can help me complete this task or take it over entirely?

- Can I complete this task without sacrificing valuable time and resources I need to spend on another professional project or personal value?
- Should I reach out to a supervisor who can advocate on my behalf for administrative support?
- Is this task actually mine or has it fallen on me because of a lack of support or direction from the administration?
- Do I need to talk to my partner about the responsibilities we share?
- Am I being drained by the sheer number of responsibilities I am carrying?

When you delegate a task, you are actually setting a boundary. Whether it's a time, emotional, or workplace boundary, drawing that line in the sand matters *because you matter.* Sometimes the person you're setting a boundary with won't understand why you're setting a boundary. That's okay. It's not necessary for everyone else to understand. You can explain why you're setting a boundary, but the other person doesn't have to affirm it for it to be valid. Your boundaries are meant to be honored and respected because you are the expert on your own life and you know what you need. Period.

## 4. Negotiate What Can Be Changed

When I worked as a VP, there were times I didn't feel I had any choice. I didn't have a choice about the meetings on my calendar, policies for my students, or budget allocations. I felt trapped by the expectations of my peers, coworkers, boss, and perhaps most suffocating, even myself. I felt alone and without control—two feelings that strongly fuel burnout. Eventually, I learned a strategy. Remember, feelings are not facts, they are information. So, when you feel alone and without choice, tell that voice it's wrong, because we always have a choice. *You* do have choices.

Throughout my years working at the college, I made choices that worked against me. But they were my choices. And I chose to stay working under their leadership. When I stayed late to work events, it was my choice. When I came into work early to prepare for a meeting, it was my choice. When work called me on my day off, I didn't have to answer. They didn't force me to pick up the phone and listen to the request. Yes, there may have been consequences, but no matter what I felt, how I acted was one hundred percent my choice. Over time, that realization helped me harness my decision-making power for my own good and according to my own values.

You have more power and influence than you think. And with that power and influence, you must advocate for yourself. No one else is going to go into your boss's office and ask him to give you the raise you deserve. No one is going to tell your husband you need a weekend away with your girlfriends. No one can do that but you. You must advocate for yourself *and* believe you have every right to. Now, before this sounds too intense, it's important to remember that this doesn't mean you have to storm into your boss's office tomorrow and demand a raise (unless you want to). You can start small. Build up your courage and confidence in your boundaries like a muscle. You can start by asking questions like the following:

- Would I be able to take off an hour early today?
- Can we push back the project that's due soon to next week?
- Is there room in the budget to support executive coaching or professional development?
- Can we schedule a meeting in the next couple of days to discuss my progress and performance?

There is no time like the present to start making intentional choices that affirm the life you want to live. Sometimes we must negotiate for what we want and no one else is going to do it for us. Stop waiting for someone to choose you. It's time to speak up and choose yourself.

## 5. Appreciate the Boundaries that Are Working

While it's important to be willing to change your life to achieve your goals, it is equally important to appreciate the boundaries that are working today. If you only look at what you can do better, your inner critic has an opportunity to step in and further distort the image you have of yourself. Acknowledging the effective boundaries you have instilled closes that negative feedback loop. If you don't acknowledge what you are doing right today, you will never think you are doing enough tomorrow. You can start by implementing these daily or weekly practices affirming what you are doing right.

### Grab the Brag Book

In case it isn't already obvious, the brag book should be your new best friend. Take some time during the day or week to write down the good things you are doing. Write out the boundaries you've set at home or work. Try to experience what it means to feel proud of yourself.

### Internally Recognize Your Impact

Take a moment at some point during your day to get quiet with yourself and remember the good you're doing. Look at how your new or existing healthy boundaries are impacting your time, energy, and well-being. For example, because you said no to that extra committee, you can take that time to go for a walk over lunch or leave work early for that workout class. It's up to you to celebrate yourself!

### Take a Quiet Moment

It can be hard to appreciate yourself with life constantly buzzing around. To combat this, take five to ten minutes to just sit with your thoughts, meditate, breathe, or journal. If your mind begins to wander, as it's prone to do, just gently redirect it back to the task at hand. Reflecting on what you've done well with your day can open room in your mind to appreciate what you're doing that's working. We must train our minds to look for the good and gratitude. It's the best antidote to burnout.

Appreciating what you're doing right can be powerful fuel for what you want to change. Knowing you're doing a good job in your current circumstances affirms you can also do a good job at the things you want to change . For myself, I knew I was a great VP. I connected well with the students and staff. My work was thorough and well done. I was good at that job. Acknowledging within myself that I was good at being a VP affirmed that I could also be great at other things, like eventually becoming an entrepreneur, keynote speaker, and leadership coach. I knew I had the skills, because I had demonstrated them in various ways throughout my career. Then I developed an internal mindset that was a game changer. It was that, with the right resources, most things we can teach ourselves. I had no reason to hold back and wait for an expert to help or give me permission.

In addition to my growing internal confidence, I also had some external motivation. I knew my kids were watching. Even though it is vulnerable and there are times I wish my kids wouldn't see all of who I am, they do. They see the organized and the messy. The calm and the stressed-out mom. The put together and the emotional woman and the confidence coach who doubts herself at times. Kids are astutely aware of how we feel about ourselves as they witness firsthand the things we say about our bodies, abilities, and how we relate this to our worth and relationships. Knowing that my journey would impact my daughters made me take a hard look at how I felt about myself. Recognizing this influence encouraged me to learn how to set boundaries in order to be the woman, leader, and mom we all deserved. My hope is that, in the future, they do the same. But instead, learn faster, set boundaries sooner, and love themselves unapologetically. It is also what I hope for you.

As you master the -ATES, I hope they help you thrive! I hope you bring these tools into your everyday life and set boundaries that perpetuate freedom and opportunity. A person who thrives is a person who creates boundaries which foster a bold and beautiful life. You deserve a bold, beautiful, and exceptional life by taking the time to set the boundaries you need to achieve the life you want to live.

When I finally set boundaries with my family and work, all our lives changed for the better. Even though it was intimidating, I shared my needs with my husband and my children. Now, my daughters know if mommy goes to her room, I'm not mad at them. I just need some alone time when I'm not being asked for a snack or touched for a few minutes. At first it can be difficult, especially when others might not understand immediately or see the benefits, but I assure you it's worth it. More often than not, my friends and family were grateful when I spoke up and asked for what I needed.

When you choose the freedom of boundaries over the fear of what could happen when you set them, you become able to be a better version of yourself.

# Chapter 6

# PSYCHOLOGICAL SAFETY IN THE WORKPLACE

IN JULY 2025, I was asked to be a keynote speaker at the *Missouri Women in Leadership Conference*. When they asked me to speak, I was almost at a loss for words. Not only were they asking me to talk about a subject I deeply cared about, but it was also a dream of mine to speak at this conference. It felt like a true full-circle moment, and I was so excited. I was also a little nervous. While I had dreamt of speaking at this conference, I knew some of the other speakers were psychologists as well. Not only was I going to be speaking to a group of people I highly respected, but I would be speaking after a group of my peers, and that was a little intimidating.

As I walked into the large conference room, I could feel the positive energy. It was an amazing surprise. There wasn't an air of competition; instead, everyone seemed to be championing their neighbor. *It was a psychologically safe space, and that felt different.* After working at a job where I was nearly the only woman in leadership, it was exciting to see so many women coming together to encourage one another and grow their confidence.

My keynote that day focused on psychological safety in the workplace. While I love every topic I speak on, psychological safety in the workplace is especially near and dear to my heart. Maybe it's because it is so directly tied to what I studied in college, or because I experienced a lack of it myself. As I developed my keynote on the topic, I created the following graphic which displays this crucial and influential concept.

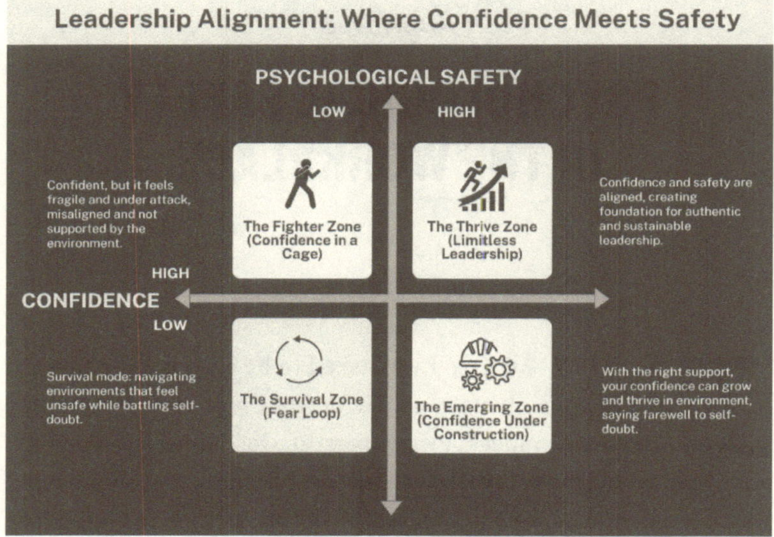



# WHAT IS PSYCHOLOGICAL SAFETY?

Psychological safety is a concept that helps us put a nuanced concept into words. I first learned about it in graduate school. Psychology in the workplace was one of my first classes in college—and my enjoyment of it seemed to signal something about what my future held. While learning about psychological safety, it made sense, but I didn't have the same fascination at the time as I did with emotional intelligence. It wasn't until I had experienced a psychologically unsafe environment that I truly absorbed and became fascinated by the material I was taught many years prior.

As an analogy, understanding what people experience in a psychologically unsafe environment is almost like how we understand a breakup. We know that when a relationship ends, there are lots of tears, sad days, and hard feelings. It is an emotional roller coaster where one person blames the other person but then also blame themselves at times. However, knowing about breakups is different than actually experiencing a breakup of your own. The same goes for psychological safety. It's one thing to know the signs, but it is altogether different to experience a psychologically unsafe environment.

Before exploring psychologically unsafe environments, let's first talk about the positive: psychological safety. To live in a psychologically safe environment means you feel free to be yourself and to speak up without fear of retaliation or retribution. As previously mentioned, we all want to feel like we belong. It's only human. In that way, psychologically safe environments foster feelings of acceptance, creativity, and belonging. On the flip side, living in a psychologically unsafe environment instead fosters burnout, shame, self-doubt, fear, and resentment.

## IDENTIFYING A PSYCHOLOGICALLY UNSAFE SPACE

Even though I knew about the importance of psychological safety, it was still difficult for me to pinpoint what I was experiencing in a psychologically unsafe environment. I was so entrenched in the toxic culture that it was hard for me to see through the fog. Maybe you're in a similar situation if you experience the following:

- In meetings, colleagues don't ask questions or share their ideas.
- There is a high turnover rate or multiple instances of quiet quitting.
- The communication style between coworkers is passive-aggressive.
- Employees avoid risk or innovation.
- There is a culture of excessive people-pleasing or perfectionism.
- Qualified candidates are passed over for a promotion, especially ones who challenge the status quo or openly disagree.
- Titles don't reflect the scope of an employee's work.
- Employees aren't paid their worth.

- There is a boss or a coworker who, for lack of better terms, tries to make your workdays hell.

I remember clearly my first "oh, wow" moment when I finally recognized I was in a psychologically unsafe space. A couple of departments were all in a meeting together. I don't remember what we were discussing, but I do remember how one of the members on the leadership team spoke to another department member. He was raising his voice, belittling the team, and scaring every other department at the same time. In that moment, I saw a different side to my leadership team—an unkind side I didn't want to interact with. I realized I was no longer in a psychologically safe environment. Admittedly, I'd witnessed several micro instances prior to this, but I would often rationalize or explain them away. After all, I was a team player. However, this instance was so blatant and uncomfortable that I could no longer ignore what was right in front of me. My body kicked into fight-or-flight mode. My anxiety shot through the roof, my sleep became a mess, and my body felt the effects.

## SYMPTOMS OF PSYCHOLOGICALLY UNSAFE ENVIRONMENTS

Once this happened, even though my body would leave work, my mind couldn't turn it off. I was stuck in a harmful cycle fueled by my psychologically unsafe environment. My mind was filled with negative self-talk. Cassie the ASSie was thriving. My pattern of hyper-independence left me feeling alone, and guilt was my constant companion. My desperate desire to be liked and safe kicked into overdrive, activating my go-to strategy of constant people-pleasing. I felt horrible, and eventually it began to show outwardly through burnout. Since I was internally struggling, my external life began to show how I was suffering. I felt an intense fear and panic due to the pressure to always be "on," to attend all events, and to show up with a smile, even when it meant missing out on important family events. I remember missing one of my daughters' first days of elementary school because there was an "important" meeting, and my husband walked her into the school solo. Later I got to hear how they were greeted by a large group of college athletes cheering them on, welcoming them on their first day. To add salt to the wound, it was a group of my college students, who were there cheering for my daughter in my absence.

Your long-term success in a workplace hinges on working in a psychologically safe environment. Without it, there is a loss of creativity, trust, and eventually your true self. Below are internal symptoms you may experience if you are working in an unsafe environment:

- Chronic stress or anxiety
- Excessive overthinking or self-doubt
- Fear of feedback or losing your job
- Physical fatigue or illness
- Withholding contributions even when you have something valuable to add

Admittedly, it can be hard to differentiate a toxic work environment from temporary challenges. However, toxic work environments are often unchanging and deeply rooted in a culture of shame and fear. Temporary challenges are difficult situations that have a clear end.

| Toxic Work Environment | Temporary Challenges |
| --- | --- |
| A coworker gossips about other employees behind their backs. | A coworker mishears what other coworkers are saying about her work. |
| A boss intentionally leaves their employee out of meetings. | After a boss leaves an organization, some employees are unintentionally left out of meetings while the company restructures. |
| A boss expects one of their employees to strictly adhere to the company's standard, while having different expectations for their other coworkers. | A boss implements new standards for their team. |
| A director intentionally overlooks an employee for a promotion when they are more than qualified because of personal reasons. | A director chooses to go with another candidate outside of the company for a promotion. |

## FROM PET TO THREAT

When new leadership started at the college, one of my bosses seemed to take a special interest in my work. I believed he liked my input and cared for my opinion. At that moment, I didn't realize he was treating me as a "pet-to-threat" employee. In the early stages, he would compliment my work, ask for advice, and even encourage my ideas. It felt nice, and I was excited to keep working with him. In the "pet" stage, bosses treat their employees well. They will dote on them and give them freedom, that is, until the employee begins surpassing the employer's expectations. As I excelled in my role, some leadership began to ignore my emails, leave me out of meetings, and belittle me in front of my coworkers. It was awful and confusing. I couldn't make sense of how my previous value was now deemed unworthy and unwanted.

The pet-to-threat leadership style operates from a base of fear instead of a place of vision. The employer is fearful that the employee will try to undermine or take their position, so the employer tries to make the employee feel weak and insecure. These types of employers tend to micromanage, name-call, and intimidate their employees. When the situation switched from treating me like an equal to calling me a "belligerent bully," it truly hurt me. Within the course of a year, a person I respected started treating me with little-to-no respect. For a time, I felt powerless. It made me believe there weren't better work environments, and if there were, they wouldn't hire someone like me. And if you have ever thought that as I did, I want you to hear me clearly and put this mantra on repeat, "It is not your fault, you deserve better, and there are still good workplaces out there."

Have you ever seen *The Intern* with Anne Hathaway and Robert De Niro? I love that movie. If you haven't seen it, warning: light spoilers ahead. There's a scene where Anne Hathaway is riding on a bike through her company. The sun is shining through the windows, the employees are smiling, and everyone seems to be having a great day. Upon initial watch, this seemed like a Hollywood mirage. Employees smiling at work? A boss who cared about the well-being of her employees? A company that cared? At the time, this all seemed completely unrealistic to me. I genuinely believed all work environments were toxic to some degree, and everyone hated their jobs at least a little bit. Since leaving my VP role, I've had the privilege of watching the movie with fresh eyes. I now know there are work environments where the employees smile more than they cry. There are environments where employees care about the person just as much as they care about successful work. There is hope for a better living situation. It's time to break the cycle.

## STEPS TO BREAK THE CYCLE

### SELF-AWARENESS

For me, breaking the cycle included going to therapy. Even therapists have therapists. We're all human, and at some point or another, all of us need help. Not only did my therapist help me understand myself better, she also helped me identify and address things that were problems that I believed were normal in my unsafe work environment. Additionally, I also did a self-audit. I would frequently find a place where I could get quiet and ask myself how I was doing.

- Have I been getting enough sleep?
- What did I do this week that fell within the realm of self-care?
- Am I taking care of my needs both physically and mentally?
- How is my relationship with my husband?
- Did I fall into people-pleasing tendencies because of my psychologically unsafe work environment?
- Have I lost my voice because of the environment I was/am in?
- Can I get it back and, if so, how?

### COMMUNICATION

After I was able to finally name work as a psychologically unsafe environment, I was ready to start communicating what needed to change. For you, this could look like reaching out to HR for help or setting up a meeting to confront the person making your environment psychologically unsafe. To build my confidence, I started modeling transparency and active listening in situations where I already felt safe.

Around this time, my team and I were in a meeting, and we watched as one of the bosses excessively verbally berated another employee. It was hard to watch, and I felt like there was nothing I could do in the moment. Yet, as we were leaving, I felt safe enough to mention how wrong the situation was. I communicated my discomfort where I felt safe. This may sound insignificant or passive, but it was my first step to addressing the problem. After I spoke up, one of my coworkers agreed. At that moment, I at least felt temporary safety. If you're in a psychologically unsafe situation, it might be a valuable first step to talk with others about your situation. Shame and fear thrive in the dark. When you share your situation with others, you are bringing it into the light where it can be better examined.

All this said, speaking out about unsafe work practices can be a double-edged sword. As you are finding those safe refuges, it's important to find a community of people who understand what you are experiencing but don't create or add to toxic gossip culture. It is helpful to know you're not alone, but it doesn't help to sit with your coworker and simply complain. We need to find supportive communities and follow up by implementing boundaries.

## BOUNDARIES

Freedom is found in the boundaries we set. When I worked at the college, I had to decide what my boundaries were going to be. Would I turn my phone on "do not disturb" at the end of the workday? Was I going to tell my team I wouldn't be able to continue working events outside my scope? This was a difficult step for me. I had to combat my natural people-pleasing tendencies, and my unhealthy perfectionism was at an all-time high because of the threatening environment. With my inner critic constantly telling me I wasn't good enough, it was hard for me to feel like I was doing anything right. But I also knew I couldn't keep living like I was. Day by day, I began to take small steps.

I started by closing my door when I needed to focus. Sometimes, I would bravely take the day off, using my vacation hours (that were already at max accrual level), and do something not work related. Some days, I did a good job speaking up for myself and my team. Other days, exhaustion and fear won out. I had to take it slow and be gracious with myself. If you or someone you know is existing in a toxic work environment, what would be some workplace boundaries you could start to implement to find or protect a psychologically safe space?

## LEADERSHIP

I knew I couldn't change the culture of the entire college overnight. However, I could focus on fostering a psychologically safe environment within my own team. My team was made up of people whom I not only trusted but who believed in our work and the students we served as much as I did. Our main focus was to help students stuck in a difficult situation. Students who lived with food insecurity. Students who were first-generation college students. Students with complicated backgrounds. Students who, frankly, reminded me a lot of myself. They were my reason to stay, and I wanted to leave them with a more than capable support system when I was gone. So, I invested where it would return dividends, in my team. The psychologically safe environment I cultivated became a haven for us and the students within the larger psychologically unsafe culture.

And while I loved the safety this provided for others, there was another benefit. When I chose to fight for a psychologically safe environment, I took a part of my life back. I was able to begin regulating my nervous system by practicing healthy habits. I started the journey of finding my way out of a constant fight, flight, or freeze response. I created the light in the tunnel I so desperately needed to see.

## SURROUND YOURSELF WITH POSITIVE FEEDBACK

When you feel like everything you do is wrong, it's important to surround yourself with people who can encourage you. While journaling and writing in my brag book was helpful, it also helped to be around people who were kind to me. Oftentimes, in psychologically unsafe situations, there is an abundance of critique and meanness. To break the cycle, I had to generate and nurture kindness. When my bosses' feedback was tainted with fearful leadership, I needed to hear kind, honest feedback from people who wanted me to succeed.

To do this, I would seek out trusted coworkers and ask for their opinions on a project I was working on. I would reach out to other women in my field and ask their advice. I knew that I was too far into a difficult internal and external situation to get out alone. To break the cycle, I needed to replace the lies with the truth. If you're in a psychologically unsafe situation, you might try out what I did to help clarify the truth of what is really going on around you and within you. You could also reach out to a leadership coach or therapist for feedback based on objective truths.

While I would never go back to working in a psychologically un-safe environment, I would be lying if I didn't acknowledge that the experience helped me learn a lot about myself. I learned how strong and resilient I can be. I learned how to pick myself up when I'd been knocked down. I've been able to sympathize and deeply understand my clients who were in similar situations. I am able to say with com-plete sincerity and in community with others, *"You're not alone and it's not your fault."*

Sadly, there are so many of us who share this experience. I've met with countless clients who work in psychologically unsafe environ-ments. Each of them is close to burnout, doesn't feel like they can trust themselves, and struggles to believe there is a place where they will feel safe. I don't judge them, because I've been them. If you believe you're in a psychologically unsafe environment, pull out a sheet of paper and answer the questions below:

- Are you able to leave the psychologically unsafe environment?
- Will you be able to take care of yourself and your responsibil-ities if you leave today?
- Do you want to leave your job?

- Are you staying at your job out of fear of the unknown?
- What limiting beliefs are you possibly believing?
- Where do you see yourself in two, five, and ten years, if you stay?
- Where do you see yourself if you decide to go?
- What is your tipping point?
- What keeps you from leaving?

Leaving a psychologically unsafe situation is usually difficult, no matter how toxic the environment is. Choosing whether to stay or go may hinge on your financial situation, the state of the economy, or how your responsibilities will shake out. Only you can weigh those options accurately. No one can tell you whether to stay or go, because no one knows you like you. When I was choosing whether to stay or leave my job, only I knew how to accurately weigh my options.

## How to Stay

There is no shame in deciding to stay where you are. But, to become healthier you do have to do something about your situation. Remember, even in staying, you have options!

- Reach out to HR for help developing a strategy, if you're able
- Invest in peer support
- Get an executive coach
- Start going to therapy
- Find your professional best friend
- Reach out to join an association aligned with your goals

While psychologically unsafe situations do have common traits, no situation is exactly the same. Take some time to know and understand what you need to start building a psychologically safe environment for yourself and your future. You need to do what feels right for you. This is also true if you decide you can no longer be in the space you are in.

## How to Go

There's no class on how you "should" leave a job. I find great joy in helping my clients develop an exit strategy they're happy with. Helping a person reclaim their power and stand in their confidence is genuinely one of my favorite aspects of my job coaching others.

For some of my clients, they want to tell their bosses to get lost and kick rocks. For others, they want to leave more subtly. I support whatever they choose. They know what they need, and I'm here to help them achieve it. For many of my clients, I encourage them to write down their version of an exit interview. In it, I tell them to write down any feedback they would give the company or even their boss directly. It's a great way to help you get quiet with yourself, process how you're feeling, and help you find closure. You also need to decide what you do and don't want to do on your way out.

When I left my job at the college, I knew I wanted certain things. I wanted to see the current Senior class graduate because I was close with many of the students. I also knew I didn't want to go to the lengthy board meetings the week after graduation. So, I planned my departure between the two. Take the time to use your vacation days. Estimate the financial impact of leaving your job. Leaving your job doesn't have to be the scary choice. You can create a plan that takes into consideration your needs, responsibilities, and financial situation.

## It's Not Your Fault

Once someone has made the decision to leave an unhealthy work environment, it's easy to look back and judge yourself for how long you stayed. Hindsight is 20/20, and sometimes it can be hard to reflect on the person you were. However, instead of judging yourself for being in an unhealthy position, the most helpful choice is to forgive yourself. You made the best choices you could with the information you had at the time. You couldn't have expected a situation to turn from healthy to hurtful, and you did not cause it. In short, it's not your fault.

For example, the way I approach work and life in general is to believe the best in people. So, when new leadership started at the college, I believed the best in them. When they betrayed my trust, I felt like I had betrayed myself in some way. Because I couldn't stop the situation from turning psychologically unsafe, I believed it was my fault. I felt responsible for a situation completely out of my control and annoyed with myself that I trusted these individuals—as though it were my fault that I didn't "know better." However, I know now that the psychologically unsafe work environment wasn't my fault. I'll say it again. If you are experiencing a psychologically unsafe environment, it isn't your fault. Sadly, it's easy to end up in an unsafe work environment; there are a lot of them out there. And, once in them, it can be difficult to feel like there is a way out. You deserve to live a life filled with hope, joy, and love. You can do this! You are brave, strong, and wonderful.

## WAIT—AM I THE BAD GUY?

Maybe you know you've not only been living in a psychologically unsafe environment, but you've been perpetuating it. This isn't an easy thing for someone to admit to themselves. So, firstly, congratulations! You have taken a huge step in the right direction by acknowledging the hurtful practices you have been encouraging. As with so many things we've discussed so far, the first step is awareness. While you might have been encouraging a psychologically unsafe environment in the past, you can start to change for the better right now. Go grab a piece of paper and ask yourself the following:

- Where did I learn to act this way?
- Am I perpetuating what I've experienced?
- What do I need to change now to better the culture?

While these are important questions, it's very important for you to get honest with yourself. You can only change what you know. Get to know yourself. Even the parts you may not like. Know that I'm proud of you and rooting for your success.

## DO YOU WANT TO DIVE DEEPER?

Throughout my time working as a leadership coach, I have noticed a general need for more information and understanding on psychological safety. If you would like more information on this topic, I implore you to check out my "Stay or Go: When Work Is No Longer Working" coaching program. This program dives deeper into psychological safety, while also giving the participant a community of people who are also navigating similar situations. If you'd like to learn more, there is information on my website.

You don't have to keep up the facade. You don't have to live in a constant state of fight-or-flight. You can live in a psychologically safe environment! You deserve to feel like you belong. Whether you stay or go is up to you but know that living in a psychologically unsafe environment is not your only option. If you'd like to change your situation, the time is now. You can do this!

# Chapter 7

# PERFECTIONISM DOESN'T WORK

**W**HEN I WAS pregnant with my first daughter, I dreamed of what kind of mom I would be. I could even picture it perfectly. I would make her baby food from organic vegetables and only feed her the most nutritious food. We would never allow screen time, only read books, and engage in Montessori activities to encourage her genius. I dreamed about buying her prom dress and celebrating her high school graduation with elaborate gifts and trips. Similarly, I prepared as best I could for what I knew would be difficult like her teenage years and potty training. I planned to solely breastfeed her. I was excited to be the best mom I could be and more to my little girl. Nine months later, my Harper was here, and she was already an amazing little girl. Maybe I'm a little biased, but can you blame me? I'm her mom, and she is my little mini-me. I thought I was ready, but unexpected difficult times came sooner than expected.

I was resolved to breastfeed my daughter. After reading the benefits of breastfeeding over formula feeding, I knew what I wanted and believed my daughter needed. I mean after all, breastmilk is colloquially called liquid gold! At the time, it seemed very straightforward to me. Then I learned more about latching. It's when the baby properly secures itself to the mother so the baby can feed. Sounds simple, right? Wrong. If you've breastfed before you know the difficulties that come with this territory—swollen breasts, soreness, and fatigue, to name a few. While I was experiencing those side effects, my daughter wouldn't latch, and my body wasn't producing enough milk. Devastating doesn't properly articulate how heartbroken I was. All I wanted was to feed my daughter, and it was the thing I couldn't do. I was stressed about my daughter getting the proper nutrition, and I blamed myself. Perfect. I had already failed as a mom—at least that was what I told myself. I literally remember crying to my mother, telling her that my daughter was going to have a lower IQ because I couldn't breastfeed her. I began to think self-defeating thoughts like, "If I can't feed my daughter, what can I ever do for her?" I was defeated, disappointed, and exhausted.

As difficult as it was, I tried to motivate myself to not give up on breastfeeding just yet. I tried every ointment, practice, and exercise I could get my hands on. I would muster as much hope as I could, try a new way to hold her or hold myself, and each time it would end with my daughter and me in tears. Despite all my best efforts, it wasn't working. I couldn't help but share my struggles with a friend, and she said the dreaded 'f' word—formula. I was hoping she would tell me something like, "No, you've got this! Keep going! Just try this vitamin, and you'll begin producing freezers of milk." If not that, I hoped at least she would tell me what I was doing wrong. I really, truly believed it was all my fault. Instead, she told me the truth: Feeding your kids formula isn't something to be ashamed of.

In a great gift of freedom and permission, she didn't reinforce the narrative that I needed to breastfeed my daughter. She told me what I needed to hear for my situation. Sometimes, kids don't want to latch, or your body doesn't make enough milk. It's going to be okay. Formula is a good thing, not something parents should be ashamed of feeding their children. I found comfort in the truth that fed is fed. My daughter was hungry, and even though formula wasn't my perfect idea of dinner for her, it would fulfill her needs. After one day of formula feeding, I couldn't remember why I was so against the idea in the first place. My daughter was laughing, full, and happy, and I felt relief for the first time in weeks. Although I believed breastfeeding was the perfect option for my daughter, I had to admit I was wrong. The idealized 'mom' in my mind was making me miserable. It wasn't until after I gave up on the idea of perfection that I could find the solution I needed.

For me, and probably many of you, perfectionism feels like a safe place. We believe, if we strive to be perfect, we can somehow achieve it, and everything will be okay. As if chasing perfection will lead us to having some kind of warped control over the situation or people stressing us out. News flash—it doesn't. Perfectionism is only a golden cage. It may look and feel nice temporarily, but you're not free.

## PERFECTIONISM DEFINED

Perfectionism is created from internal and social pressures to perform and appear without fault. This is then further fueled by fear of judgment, rejection, failure, disappointing others, shame, or losing control. Perfectionists use their perfectionism to gain approval, control, or safety. And while it can seem excellence driven, it's rooted in shame and fear. For many, perfectionism takes root early in life since it's established and fostered in environments where love, approval, or safety feel conditional. To gain control over those fears of losing those things, a person strives to live a perfect life.

To return to the example of breastfeeding, I felt like my success as a mother was found in being able to breastfeed my daughter. My perfectionism attached itself to this idea and fed my fear that I wouldn't be able to be a good mother if I didn't breastfeed her. This perfectionism fed my greatest fears and held me back from what the best version of success looked like for me.

Perfectionism, like other fear-driven mindsets, is like a weed. While it's very easy for a weed to take root, it's difficult to remove. As a person who grew up in an unstable home, my "soil" made me more prone to falling into a perfectionist's mindset. Since I only saw my father during the summers, I wanted him to see me as the perfect daughter in the limited time we had together. I wanted him to love and be proud of me, so I ran toward perfectionism. It felt like a safe place for me to land, but little did I know, it was fostering a toxic mental state. There are many environments where perfectionism commonly takes root and thrives. Environments like the following:

- In early childhood where love was conditional
- From trauma, instability, or unpredictability in someone's life
- In shame-based family systems
- From cultural or gender-based expectations

The outward expression of perfectionism looks a little different for everyone who lives with it. For me, in the breastfeeding example, it manifested as feeling like I had to practice traditional maternal roles with my daughters to be a successful mom. While every perfectionist executes it differently, the core traits of perfectionists are similar.

## COMMON TRAITS OF A PERFECTIONIST

- Sets unrealistically high standards
- Is excessively self-critical
- Avoids risks or new experiences unless there is guaranteed success
- Struggles with delegation
- Carries a deep fear of failure or making mistakes
- Procrastinates due to fear of not doing something "right"
- Links self-worth to success
- Engages in black-and-white thinking
- Has an overactive inner critic

Of course, no one strives to practice any of the above. But it can be easy to rationalize the downsides of a perfectionist's mindset with the short-term perks. When I was a practicing perfectionist, I truly didn't believe it was that bad. I was seen as successful, driven, and hard working. These were all things I wanted to be known for, but I didn't realize the long-term effects were looming. After years of living in the fear of failing at perfectionism, I started to feel its harmful effects.[5]

| Short-Term Perks | Long-Term Effects |
| --- | --- |
| Verbal praise and rewards for high performance | Disconnection from your authentic self |
| A sense of control and predictability | Procrastination or paralysis |
| The ability to feel "productive" | Difficulty enjoying success or feeling "enough" |
| Initial approval and validation from others | Strained relationships |
| Temporary relief from anxiety or self-doubt | Chronic stress, burnout, and anxiety |

These negative long-term effects are nearly unavoidable because perfectionism demands performance instead of authentically living, acting, and connecting. It erodes confidence because your worth is directly tied to your performance. What I thought was protecting the life I wanted to live actually was integral in unravelling it. When I was scared to apply to the VP position at the college, perfectionism lived at the front of my mind telling me I wasn't good enough. And while I'm proud of myself for pushing through perfectionism in that instance, I didn't always do it. I let perfectionism hold me back from plenty of opportunities I could've had out of fear.

According to an internal Hewlett Packard Study referenced in Sheryl Sandberg's infamous book *Lean In,* women only apply to jobs where they meet 95–100 percent of the job requirements.[5] In conjunction, men apply to jobs where they only meet at least 60 percent of the role's requirements. In short, women are more willing to self-reject than men if they feel they are not "fully qualified." This research shows that a commitment to perfectionism and fear are literally robbing women of opportunity. And it affects not only our futures. It can be actively hurting us today.

While each of those listed long-term consequences of perfectionism are hurtful, I believe the disconnection from self is the most damaging. The others—decision paralysis, difficulty enjoying success, and chronic burnout—can all stem from a disconnection of self.

For me, this even looked like feeling the need for the perfect body. When I was at my unhealthiest mentally, perfectionism overload, I was also at my heaviest weight. I've been very transparent about my physical health journey, because I believe it's so closely linked to our mental health. When I was anxious every day and striving for the perfect life, my body was 90 pounds heavier. I felt physically and mentally awful.

Then when I finally started to break down why I felt the need to be perfect, I became better able to manage my anxiety. In doing so, it helped me with my relationship with my body. I was also able to let go of ideas related to the "perfect" number on the scale, extremes related to "good" and "bad" food, and guilt and shame related to eating. At the root of perfection is an internal struggle and striving for control, which sometimes we apply to other areas of our life like our body, relationships, and work. By better managing my anxiety, letting go of this notion of perfection, and relinquishing unhealthy control, I broke free from shame and guilt that kept me stuck. I was able to let my body know it didn't need to live in fight, flight, or freeze mode. I was able to take back my body. You will likely have similar personal results when you begin to push back against the drive for perfectionism.

Perfectionism doesn't just affect your relationship with yourself. It also steals from your relationships with others. It wasn't until I started to deconstruct the perfect 'mom' from my head that I was able to truly show up for my daughter. While I carried unrealistically high standards for myself, I also inadvertently carried those unspoken un-realistic expectations for others. The same perfectionist expectations you hold for yourself, you will inevitably hold for others, no matter how much you may try not to.

For example, when living in a perfectionist mindset, you might start to resent friends or family when unspoken expectations are left unmet. Perfectionism also reduces vulnerability and intimacy in relationships out of fear of rejection. It creates pressure, control, and sometimes distance, while making it harder to ask for help or receive love unconditionally. Again, while I initially believed striving for perfectionism would make my relationships thrive, it was actually straining them. True excellence comes with flexibility, self-trust, and a willingness to push against rigidness or fear of failure.

## PERFECTIONISM DOESN'T EXIST ALONE

In my journey to understand and dismantle my perfectionist mindset, I found myself simultaneously working on my people-pleasing ten-dencies. Perfectionism sometimes disguises itself as other practices like people-pleasing since they do have certain traits in common. Yet they are not the same.

Perfectionism can easily be confused with high achievement, having a strong work ethic, paying attention to detail, ambition, or responsibility—that's part of what makes it so hard to stop. It does such a good job of masking fear and offering seemingly positive results that it's hard for a person to believe they would be able to be successful without it. However, perfectionism also encouraged my inner critic. Our inner critic and perfectionism operate from a place of fear and in-adequacy and use shame as a motivator. In this way, my perfectionism and inner critic undermined my confidence and self-trust, amplified my self-judgment, and minimized my accomplishments. They were the very loud voices that perpetuated the belief I wasn't good enough.

As mentioned, women are more prone to perfectionism due to being taught from an early age to internalize societal expectations around performance, appearance, motherhood, and success. The pressure to do it all and to do it flawlessly is then further compounded with systemic bias, cultural messaging, and lack of representation. Since women are socialized to be more communicative and others-focused than men, it leads them to compare themselves more often to others' more "perfect" lives. And as I've worked with hundreds of women, I've found three places where perfectionism most commonly thrives.

- "Superwoman" (a.k.a. I can do it all!) Perfectionism
  - She tries to be everything to everyone.
- Appearance-Based Perfectionism
  - The woman who wants to be seen as beautiful according to what she believes society wants her to be.
- Emotional Perfectionism
  - She never wants to be seen as angry. Instead, she wants to be viewed as always kind and available.

Do you see yourself in any of these descriptions? They all are strategies to feel approval and safety from others.

## WOMEN CAN HAVE IT ALL

Raise your hand if you've ever heard the saying, "Women can have it all." Of course it sounds nice, but do we really want it all? Men are rarely told they can or should have it all, so why do we sometimes believe we are failing if we don't? And what does having it all really mean? While the phrase can sound empowering, it is yet another part of our cultural messaging that reinforces the practice of perfectionism. It implies we should excel in every role, space, and relationship without struggle or support. It paints a false picture of what is possible or what we even "should" want.

Instead of striving to have it all, what we can actually strive for is to live lives full of joy, purpose, and love—and *not* at the cost of your authenticity and mental health. I've had so many clients who have had to process through the false pretense of having it all. I've coached countless women who have been on the verge of panic attacks and lived with extreme anxiety over a meeting, interview, or presentation that might result in something that does not fit that idealized picture. And I always tell them the same thing—your worth isn't up for debate, and your value isn't in your output.

In addition, I also ask them a couple of questions. Go ahead and pull out a sheet of paper and ask yourself the following:

- Who do you trust and admire?
- What do you really want in your life?
- What is perfectionism costing you in your career, relationships, and relationship with self?
- Who do you feel more comfortable with: the perfect person in the room or the authentic one?

When I my daughters first started school, I didn't believe I could be friends with whom I deemed "the Pinterest moms." These moms would make everything from birthday decorations to cookies to Halloween costumes from scratch. They were everything I wanted to be, and I was nothing like them. I know now that my reaction was because I was operating from a place of fear and I was intimidated by their seemingly perfect lives.

Since they lived lives veiled in perfectionism, I instead gravitated toward the moms who lived authentically. For example, one morning a dear friend was running out the door to take her kids to school. On the way out, she thought she grabbed a soda. While in the drop-off line, she absentmindedly opened the can and took a drink. Immediately she spit it out, realizing she hadn't grabbed a soda but instead an alcoholic beverage. She immediately threw it away, and when she told the story, I understood and laughed with her. Parenting is hard and sometimes you accidentally grab the wrong can.

The beautiful part was that my friend could've kept this imperfect story to herself, but instead she shared. In her sharing her imperfect story, I found comfort and comradery. The Pinterest moms' lives were appealing from the outside, but the authentic moms were the ones living lives grounded in confidence. After my friend shared her story, I felt more comfortable sharing my own imperfect moments with others, allowing me to grow in confidence along the way. What could sharing your imperfect stories do for you?

## Are You a Perfectionist?

When living as a perfectionist, I didn't recognize the reality of my situation. Honestly, if you would have asked me if I thought I was a perfectionist, I probably wouldn't have believed it was a serious issue to address. It wasn't until after many conversations and acknowledging my consistent burnout that I realized maybe my perfectionism wasn't a superpower. Maybe this is true for you as well. Maybe you're sitting and reading this thinking, "I'm not a perfectionist. I'm just a high achiever."

Take out a piece of paper and ask yourself the following.

- Do I tie my worth to what I achieve?
- Do I fear making mistakes or being judged?
- Do I procrastinate out of fear of not doing it "right"?
- Do I rarely feel satisfied even when I succeed?
- Do I overlook or over-prepare to feel "safe"?
- Do I avoid feedback because I absorb anything critical as a failure?

If you answered yes to any of the above, you are living in a perfectionist mindset. But don't worry! Acknowledging the problem is the first step. Now, it's time to combat the issue.

# HOW TO STOP LIVING IN A PERFECTIONIST MINDSET

The tonic for perfectionism is self-compassion, authenticity, acceptance, and flexibility. These elements allow you the freedom to grow with space for imperfection, humanity, and trust.

## SELF-COMPASSION

Grab your journal and start chronicling moments when you were hard on yourself. In tandem, grab your brag book and describe times when you successfully showed yourself compassion. Note the difference in how you felt, treated yourself, and interacted with others based on those responses.

## GET CURIOUS

To break through the fear of failure, slowly start trying new things. Maybe that looks like joining a cooking or dance class. Maybe it looks like trying a new kind of workout. I would even encourage you to do something you think you'll be bad at even if it's just in the privacy of your own home! My guess is you will surprise yourself or at least get some good laughs in.

## EXPLORE

In therapy, I was able to ask myself, "Where did these beliefs about perfectionism come from?" Also, "What would it look like to be 'good enough' instead of 'flawless'?" And while I appreciated going to therapy and highly recommend it, your journey of exploration may not look the same. Additional avenues for exploration include journaling, talking with friends, or simply creating the space and silence that allows you to sit and ponder. Regardless of how you go about it, combating perfectionism requires that you find a way to get to the root of why you believe and behave the ways you do.

## SET IMPERFECT GOALS

Take a second and grab another piece of paper or create a section in your journal to make a goal—any kind of goal. Maybe you want to start going to more concerts or start your own business. Set the goal and then pause to consider and accept that the execution of this goal may not look exactly like you pictured. If you set a goal to finish a project by the end of the year, great! But also, give yourself room to know that it's okay if you don't perfectly complete the goal in that time. You're human. Do your best and let go of the rest.

Much like many of you, as much as I had convinced myself that perfectionism was a badge of honor, I eventually had to concede it was actually a barrier. Perfectionism tied my worth to what I earned or accomplished, and it made me feel worthless when I "failed." I know now that my worth isn't rooted in what I've done. It's rooted in who I am. You are inherently valuable and your mistakes will never take that away. In truth, your acceptance of yourself and others as limited humans can actually enhance your voice, impact, and leadership. In my example, when I chose to be the mom I was over the mom I wanted to be, I was exactly the mom my daughter needed. And when you choose the person you want to be, you will also become what you and others really need. Choosing to be real over perfect is where freedom and confidence thrive, and that is where you want to be.

# Chapter 8

# APPRECIATING OUR BODIES

**Y**EARS OF BUYING into perfectionism led me to believe that I had to be perfect at everything—including having the perfect body. Ever since I was a little girl, I've been conscious of how other people perceive my physical appearance. This awareness became especially strong in sixth grade. Like every other year in elementary school, we had gym class. Sometimes we would play games, and other days we would see how many pushups we could do. On this day, our teacher had us run some laps. While I was running around the gym, I noticed some of the kids were pointing at me. And while the pointing was bad enough, they were also laughing. I then realized they were laughing at the way my body moved while I was running. I immediately felt ashamed and embarrassed. I wanted to run into the locker room and never come out. At that moment, I had no ability or perspective to be confident in who I was or the healthy activity I was doing with my body. I just desperately wanted to be like the cool kids.

When I was in school, the cool kids were the athletes. They were tall, thin, and winners. I was an uncoordinated girl with divorced parents who didn't push athleticism or healthy habits. I was also surrounded by relatives who were constantly talking about the new diet they wanted to try or their "problem areas." And while they were focused on criticizing their bodies, they inadvertently taught me to do the same. As an easily influenced young girl, these messages affirmed the lie that my worth was tied to how I look. This was a lie I would believe for a very long time.

As you've learned, growing up, I didn't feel like I was enough. I leaned into people-pleasing and perfectionism to make me feel like I was worth something. These beliefs then encouraged me to develop an unhealthy, unkind, abusive, and complicated relationship between myself and how I viewed my body. It didn't help that the parental figures in my life weren't focused on long-term physical health either. I don't fault them for it—they were just doing what they had learned from their parents and simply focused on surviving.

As a child, it didn't seem all bad, and I have some lovely, warm memories from the times our family spent together around food. My granny made the most amazing dinners with real butter and paired them perfectly sweetened juice and tea. Do you remember those big popcorn tins? She would have one of those on her counter filled with sugar and would pull out that tin for every meal. One time, I remember eating SpaghettiOs at my mom's house and thinking it tasted nothing like Granny's. I later discovered Granny had been adding sugar to the SpaghettiOs she had been serving my brother and me. Suffice it to say, sugar has always been a staple in my family meals.

Years later in my PhD program, I learned about the mental toll that results from a negative body image. And even with that education, I've struggled. I have literally tried almost every diet there is, from Weight Watchers, Jenny Craig, Medifast (my least favorite), Paleo, Whole 30, Atkins, and the list goes on and on. After years of practicing hating my body, I couldn't fathom simply appreciating it. It just seemed like one of those battles I would never win.

It wasn't till years later, after having my daughters, that I joined a coaching program. Although I'd already lost some weight with medication, I hadn't done the real work, like addressing my relationship with my body, food, the scale, etc. This program was what finally helped me truly understand my situation, guilt and shame cycle, and the negative criticism I perpetuated about the body I frequently tried to hide. I also realized an important, comforting lesson—I wasn't alone. Women all around me struggle with the exact same things.

Since my years learning in graduate school, many researchers have furthered the studies on the impacts of a negative or positive body image. Some of what they have found links our feelings about our bodies to social media influence, comments from adults, and feelings of pride or shame. To give a little more perspective, please consider the statistics below:

- 87 percent of women report some level of dissatisfaction with their bodies.[6]
- 73 percent of adult women reported being either heavier or lighter than their ideal body.[7]
- 50 percent of teen girls use unhealthy weight control behaviors.[8]
- It has been estimated that the average woman criticizes her appearance at least eight times a day in the mirror.

This type of research also confronted me with the reality of the long-term positive and negative effects that are tied to how we view ourselves.

| Effects of a Negative Mindset | Effects of a Positive Mindset |
| --- | --- |
| Chronic stress-related illness | Greater emotional resilience |
| Relationship difficulties such as intimacy avoidance and consistent insecurity | Healthier relationships |
| Depression and anxiety | Increased willingness to care for your body, such as taking the time to exercise |
| In some cases, self-harm, substance abuse, or eating disorders | Reduced risk of developing an eating disorder |

| Low self-worth | Stronger self-confidence and self-advocacy |
| --- | --- |
| Loss of time, energy, and joy from obsessing over appearance | Mental and physical freedom to better focus on what matters to you |

When I first learned the statistics, they shook me to my core. Not only was I one of the 91 percent of women dissatisfied with my appearance, but I was also raising two little girls. Harper, my eldest, is a great mirror. She challenges me to think and to examine my behaviors, thoughts, and words. And of course, I only want the absolute best for her. I remember, late one evening, I was bathing her. Harper looked at me, asked me to sit down, and said she was worried because, "I don't want to be fat like you, Mommy." While she couldn't understand how harsh she was being, she also knew she didn't want to look like me. Thankfully, by this point, I had worked through a generous portion of my negative body image. In this moment, I looked back at my smart girl and told her the truth.

Mommy doesn't see herself as fat or big (these are also words we do not use in my house as they are unkind). Mommy sees herself as strong. I also told her I grew her little sister and herself in my tummy, which is really freaking cool. My body is shaped the way it is not only because of how I was made, but also because I carried her. I ended the conversation by telling her I love my body, and I meant it.

In a beautiful moment, Harper then broke into a sweet smile and told me she loves my tummy, and that she wasn't scared anymore. I told her I think she is kind and wonderful. She quickly went back to playing with her many Barbies that were swimming in the bathtub. I was grateful to be able to talk with her the way I wish my mom had spoken with me when I was little. A generation later, I now have the privilege to be able to introduce to her the idea that she should be proud of what she does, not how her body looks while doing it. And the same goes for you!

# OUR MENTAL HEALTH AND OUR BODY

While I was working at the college, I became pregnant with my second daughter, Lauren. Unlike with my first daughter, when I went in for my blood sugar test, the doctor told me I had gestational diabetes. In short, it's a type of diabetes that only develops when pregnant. When I learned my prognosis, I was devastated. My perfectionism told me it was all my fault, and again, I struggled with thoughts of being a horrible mother. I now know that gestational diabetes isn't directly tied to the mother's weight, but back then, it was a difficult situation for me to understand. This diagnosis also triggered a deep-rooted fear of mine—that I would have health issues like my mom. I guess Harper and I aren't so different. Yet, as scared as I was, there was a bright side. This diagnosis encouraged me to learn more about the food I was putting in my body. I learned fruit spikes my blood sugar more than expected, and some foods I deemed healthy were actually negatively affecting me. As I learned about the effects of certain foods on my body, I was encouraged because it broke through a lie I had believed for a very long time. The lie that my body was incapable of change.

Since leaving the college, my husband and I decided our family was complete. In turn, I realized there were no more excuses. My body wasn't going to change anymore from pregnancy, and I was tired of hating my body. One day while sharing my struggles with a friend, she told me about her own health journey. She also shared her experience with a weight loss management drug—GLP-1 medication. Later, I shared her experience with my doctor, who thought it may be just what my body needed. And while a GLP-1 medication may not be for everyone, it was for me.

My experience with this medication meant that, finally, my food noise was silenced, and I was able to make it through the day without constantly worrying about the food I was eating and how it was affecting my body. Food noise is like the evil stepsister to the inner critic. Like the inner critic, its goal is to make you feel insecure about every choice you make, but it's specifically focused on your body and food. When the GLP-1 medication silenced my food noise, it seemed like a kind of miracle, and I was finally able to think clearly about my food choices.

When I look back over the last couple of years, I think about days when I saw the scale go down and smile. I think about trying on dresses that used to be tight that started to fit like a glove. Of course, losing weight felt great, but it was only part of the puzzle. The real confidence when I started to truly change my mindset.

## WORKING THROUGH FEAR AND SHAME

It's no secret that women's bodies have long been hypersexualized. However, it seems like there is also an unspoken professional rule associated with women's bodies—if you're not seen as physically healthy, people don't trust you to lead a team. It's ridiculous. How we look doesn't affect how we lead, but our cultural standards lead us to believe there is a correlation. When I started my health journey, even though I knew those standards were unfair and untrue, I still had to break down those beliefs. I had to realize they were rooted in fear.

In your relationship with your body, are you hiding yourself out of fear? Take a moment, grab a sheet of paper, and answer the questions below:

- How do you feel in your body?
- Do you wear certain clothes to hide parts of your body?
- What clothes make you feel good?
- Why do they make you feel good?

How you feel in what you wear is how you will show up. After years of hiding in clothes that were not really "me," I've found I love living in bright colors, specifically bold pinks, reds, and fun patterns. When

I was at an uncomfortable weight, I would dream of wearing certain fashionable "louder" outfits, that perfect pair of jeans, or a bathing suit, but I felt the need to hide my body. Because I have done the inner work, I feel more able to express my love of fashion and wear clothes beyond the black pants and black shirt uniform. Wearing brighter or more fashionable clothes makes me feel confident, so I now exude more confidence at events and in relationships. I am hopeful that as you explore your own relationship with your body and how you present yourself, you may experience some of the same benefits, finding your unique style.

## STRESS AFFECTS YOUR WHOLE BODY

At the core of my health issues was the reality that I was stuck in a fear mindset. Constantly living with this level of stress routinely activated my hypothalamic-pituitary-adrenal (HPA) axis. This means the chemicals in your brain are activating your cortisol, the stress hormone, which makes your body feel like it's in fight-or-flight mode, regardless of whether you are actually in danger. Consistently experiencing a high level of cortisol in your body leads to inflammation, hormone dysregulation, and weakened immunity which, in turn, affects sleep, digestion, and energy. And I was shocked to learn, it affects how your body stores fat. When you're in fight-or-flight mode, your body believes you'll need the extra fat to survive, so it stores it.

However, when you bring yourself out of fight-or-flight mode, your body is better able to function as it should. When I worked at the college, my mind was in near constant fight or flight, and so was my body. In those days, I used food to cope with my stress. Food gave me a positive dopamine hit. When I worked in that psychologically unsafe environment, food became something that made me feel good. So, I constantly reached for it. Since leaving my toxic workplace, I've lost ninety pounds. And while I did start a GLP-1 medication,

I don't believe I would've been able to lose the weight I did without leaving that work environment. My body was constantly stressed to the max, and I know my mind lived in fight-or-flight mode. After leaving my toxic work environment, my body (and my relationship with it) changed for the better.

Are you using food or other substances to help you cope with a difficult situation? Using food to cope with stress disconnects us from the messages our bodies are trying to send us. Simply said, when we're disconnected from our bodies, it becomes easier to fall into disordered eating habits.

## EATING DISORDERS

While I was in my PhD program, I learned about disordered eating habits and eating disorders. To be clear, an eating disorder is a psychological disorder like anorexia or bulimia. However, disordered eating habits are various habits that encourage an eating disorder. When I was working as a VP, I met with many students who partook in some kind of disordered eating habit. Usually, I saw students also abuse alcohol in tandem with a disordered eating habit. I distinctly remember when some young women told me they wouldn't eat dinner so they would later be able to feel a buzz from the alcohol faster. It broke my heart to see them reinforce a disordered eating habit in this way.

For years, women have been more likely to have an eating disorder than men. At their core, eating disorders are a type of control management. Perhaps as you're reading this, you're wondering if you are living with an eating disorder. If you know or suspect that you are please know this: you're not alone, and people want to help you. You can find help from a therapist or the National Alliance for Eating Disorders, but you are already taking a step in the right direction by admitting you are struggling.

Or maybe, you're witnessing someone who is living with an eating disorder. It can be difficult to know how to speak to that person. One of the best places to start is by having a conversation with them filled with compassion, not judgment. Starting conversations with, "You need to stop doing this," will not lead to the results you want. Instead, carefully raise concern about certain disordered eating patterns you have noticed. Ask how you can support them. Let them know you will be with them each step of the way and seek out helpful resources. While eating disorders develop to help someone feel in control, they ultimately will only erode and destroy your life. If you or someone you know is struggling, know that you can overcome it.

# HOW TO GET OFF THE ROLLER COASTER

For a long time, I believed I wouldn't ever be able to feel content or happy with my body. The journey with my body felt like I was on a roller coaster filled with highs and lows. Now, I love my body not just for how it looks but for what it does for me. And you can feel the same. It's time to get off the roller coaster and live in freedom. It starts with awareness.

## AWARENESS

Identifying what is making you feel self-conscious about your body is the first step. For myself, this looked like going through my closet and finding which clothes made me feel uncomfortable and which ones boosted my confidence. Then, after you identify the problem, you can start to practice small acts of kindness. As an example, when I found that I hated wearing the color navy, I erased the color from my closet. For you, this might look like learning to love your scale as it is just a number and not a reflection of your worth. Maybe it's resting without guilt or unfollowing some toxic social media accounts. Take a moment to ask yourself: What is a small act of kindness I can give myself today that will improve my relationship with my body?

## Practice a Self-Talk Audit

If you can only see what you hate about yourself, you must address that first. To my clients, I recommend they take a head-to-toe scan of themselves. After you're done, go ahead and say everything you hate and love about your body. It's okay. You may start with the negative, but along the way, you will find at least one thing you like about yourself. In my case, I have always been insecure about my midsection, but I have learned to appreciate that I held two babies in there, which is magical. When I did this, I was delighted to find I liked the color of my eyes, my smile, and the way my legs are toned. When you start liking one part about yourself, you start to notice other parts of yourself you like as well. Some prefer to do a self-talk audit in front of a mirror and out loud, while others like writing it in a journal. Find what works best for you.

## Curating Your Input

As you're working on your body confidence, it's also important to surround yourself with positive influences. Let's take Elyse, for example. Elyse has been working on her body confidence for over six months, and she is proud of her progress. Now, she feels ready to intentionally add healthy habits and discard the habits that were no longer serving her long-term goals. Unfortunately, she can't distance herself from every trigger because of her job that she is currently unable to leave. However, she can start by adding good influences to her social media rotation. Maybe you're in a similar predicament. Take a moment and ponder: What are some good influences you can add to your life? For myself, I started following social media influencers whose content focused on body appreciation. I also invested in growing a community that understood what I was going through. I joined a coaching program for women called the Yummy Mummy Experience. In this program, I was able to connect with other women who had struggled with their weight, while also learning new tools, backed in psychology, to work on my inner dialogue. I also found community in sharing with my friends and other women about my weight loss journey.

Additionally, I also recommend that you surround yourself with people who not only love you, but do so unconditionally. And when you are with your people, let them know what kinds of support you need. When first I started my health journey, I told my husband I needed to focus on my own health needs. It didn't work out for us to do the same exercises or eat the same way, but he was able to support me nonetheless. You may also find community in a local gym, a Facebook group, or from a health coach. Regardless of where you find your community, be intentional, and focus on body appreciation. Invest in your support community and allow them to encourage you on hard days and possibly even introduce you to new practices to help you reconnect with your body.

## Reconnect with Your Body

When you're ready, it's time to flip your body mindset. A great way to do that is through mirror work. Get up and stand in front of a full-length mirror. Take a couple of deep breaths and then say what you love about yourself. There's no need to rush, so feel free to take as much time as you need. The more you do it, the easier it will be, and the more affirmed you will be in how beautiful you really are.

Connecting with your body also looks like intentional movement. This step looks a little different to everyone. I love an early-morning walk with my puppy, Delta Dawn, and a weighted vest. It may also look like a Peloton, CrossFit, or yoga class. Maybe it looks the same for you, or it could be a hike. It could be a HIIT class or intentional stretching. Be willing to try different kinds of movement until you find a type that fits your lifestyle and needs. Reconnecting with your body is found in bringing your mind and body to the same place in a spirit of appreciation. Just start somewhere. You've got this!

## GOOD THINGS TAKE TIME

At this point I want to make sure to tell you, my health journey wasn't and isn't linear. Some of my hardest days were spent feeling helpless, heavy, uncomfortable, and unsure what to do about my body. At times, I felt my discomfort knew no end, like when I had to buy bigger clothes or ask for a seat belt extender on flights. I will never forget the pure gut-wrenching embarrassment I felt as I exited a roller coaster ride because the seat belt wouldn't secure. I won't sugarcoat it. I felt awful, but I had to push forward. Maybe you're feeling the same way. Maybe you feel behind or exhausted. It's okay. In these moments, it's a great time to get honest with yourself.

If you feel behind, ask yourself: What is my timeline rooted in? Or maybe you need to ask yourself more logistical questions. Is your diet holding you back more than encouraging your health journey? If you're exhausted, take the time you need to rest. Reevaluate your goals and learn to be okay with living on a different timeline than the people around you. If you're working through a perfectionist mindset, this is a great time to practice setting imperfect goals! Test new workouts, recipes, routines, and lifestyles. Be willing to have bad days. While you should expect your life to change for the better during your health journey, you can also expect to experience some hard feelings and hard days. Because that's a real, unperfect life.

Remember, your feelings are information to be considered with curiosity. If you feel sad after taking a walk every day, maybe you need to try something else that elicits more positive feelings. You can practice using the container method we learned about in the emotional intelligence chapter to process what you're feeling. Try journaling how you feel and don't judge yourself. Keep going. The hard days won't last forever.

# THERE'S A BETTER WAY TO LIVE

I want to be very clear. If you want to change the way you look or carry yourself, you can. Just make sure it's rooted in what you want for yourself, not what you believe someone else prefers. In this life, we are only given one body. If you're not taking care of it, you're not able to show up as your best self in any aspect of your life. If you're shrinking who you are, you're not living in confidence. You deserve to live a happy life brimming with confidence from the inside out. The freedom you will feel when you love your body is worth pursuing. Lifelong confidence is worth your time. Now, it's time to take that confidence and lead others.

Chapter 9:

# LEADING WITH CONFIDENCE

ESPITE A LONG history with perfectionism and self-confidence issues, I have always had a rather audacious personality and been willing to make daring choices. And while some of these choices were fun, others were made because I was between a rock and a hard place. It was in one of these latter situations when I decided to make one of the most daring decisions of my life.

For years, I tried to be a flexible kid. I tried to be the "good girl" who helped her mom pack up the kitchen for a move, even though I had just made some new friends. I was willing to wear a fake smile in the car and hide my tears for years. Moving was always hard, but it was easier when I was little. It was easier to believe I would make new friends or find my place again. As I grew older, I realized making friends is hard and finding a place where you fit is rare. So, when I felt happy where I was, I wasn't ready to just give it up. Then, when I was sixteen, my mom came to me and let me know she was getting married and we could not continue living with her. I was faced with a choice: I could put on a fake smile, or I could stand up for myself. At this point, she had already decided that my brother and I were going to live with my dad in Texas.

I knew I didn't want my life to change again, as it was toward the end of my high school career. Unfortunately, whether I chose to move in with my dad or not, I had to accept that my life was going to change. I couldn't control that, but I could decide how much I wanted my life to change. So, I reached out to a friend and let her know my situation. She heard my concerns, and we devised a plan to ask her parents if I could move in with their family. Her parents were so incredibly gracious and welcomed me into their home, where I got my own bedroom. They even let me paint it a beautiful shade of lilac. Unfortunately, that friendship eventually went south, as is common when you're sixteen years old. Yet again, I had to find another option.

Enter another friend who was old enough to sign a lease and knew my situation. While some kids were getting their driver's licenses, I was signing my first lease. Perfect! I told my mom and dad, who took it better than expected, and I was ready to go into the world on my own. The plan sounded simple enough: work to pay rent while finishing high school. I was resolved to figure it out. Even though I was afraid of living on my own at such a pivotal age, I wanted to take back control and start living my life the way I wanted to. This is the mindset of someone who leads with confidence. It's being willing to choose the unknown and figure it out along the way—despite being afraid. Of course, when I was sixteen, I wouldn't have said I was leading with confidence. I probably would've downplayed my effort and made some kind of passing remark, making it no big deal. I didn't quite realize what I was doing.

Today, I look back with love for that girl. The girl who was willing. The girl who knew what she wanted and trusted herself even when she was scared. Yet somehow, I lost part of that girl along the way. I slowly chipped away at that part of myself when I compromised with people-pleasing tendencies and chose to live as a chameleon instead of my authentic self. It wasn't until I was in my thirties working at the college that I realized I wanted to make my way back to that girl. I was ready to be the woman who stood up for herself and advocated for her needs. I was tired of being a woman who shrank herself to fit into the mold society had designed for her. I was ready to lead with confidence grounded in self-trust instead of fear.

So, I focused on growing my self-confidence and read books on emotional intelligence. I started working with a therapist and grew my community. Eventually, I began to feel like that audacious sixteen-year-old: confident. In turn, I felt emboldened to stand up for myself and resolved to set boundaries at work. When I decided I wanted to pivot from my C-suite position to being a leadership coach and keynote speaker, I was faced with two choices. I could stay at the place I knew, or I could choose the scarier option and figure it out along the way. Again, I made the scarier choice, and today, I couldn't be happier.

Up to this point, we have been focused on specific areas that drain or boost our confidence. Leading with confidence is what happens when you start living out these principles from the previous chapters. Now it's time to take what I've taught you so far and start living!

## CONFIDENCE IS CONTAGIOUS

Most contagions we try to avoid, but not confidence. If you're going to catch something from someone, this is what you want. Like I've said, confidence isn't a trait. *It's a skill.* And it's a skill that we can rub off on each other. When you lead with confidence, you are showing the people around you they can also be confident. There is a kind of communal hope factor associated with confidence. It's why I believe representation is so important. When women see other women living with confidence, the air in the room shifts for the better. It's important to me that my daughters see me as confident. I want them to know within their bones that they can be confident in who they are because they've seen it lived out. Additionally, there are a number of positive psychological outcomes that result from confidence.

When a person is confident, they are more willing to build trust, increase their influence, and inspire fellowship. In general, a confident leader is more effective than a fearful leader. We want to be in places and near people who make us feel safe, and confidence makes us feel safe. No truly confident leader has to announce, "I'm confident!" We can see it in the way they communicate and hold themselves.

| Leading with Confidence | Leading Without Confidence |
| --- | --- |
| They clearly communicate expectations without apologizing. | They over-explain or frequently apologize. |
| They are grounded in their values, choosing to lead from a place of integrity over fear. | They choose to people-please to avoid conflict. |
| Their body language conveys strength. | They choose to stay silent in meetings despite having good ideas. |
| There is a willingness to make decisions even if they are difficult. | There is a hesitation or second-guessing when they are trying to make decisions. |
| They are vulnerable and willing to admit to mistakes, ask for help, or invite collaboration. | They are closed off and defensive when given criticism. |

We all want to follow people who are confident. When I was working at the college, I initially enjoyed working for my boss because he exhibited the traits of a person leading with confidence. I felt safe working there until the new leadership stepped in. Then I found myself shrinking in meetings, staying silent, and I ended up burned out. Whether you're in a similar situation or not, you can take steps to build up, reinforce, or secure a mindset steadfast on leading with confidence. But before you do that, I want to make sure to highlight just a few other things that can prevent us from leading with the confidence we desire. One that tripped me up for a long time was impression management.

## IMPRESSION MANAGEMENT

For as long as I can remember, I've wanted people to like me. And while this isn't inherently wrong, I regularly went too far, willing to morph myself into whatever the other person wanted me to be so they would like me. I would use people-pleasing, chameleon, or perfectionism tools to manage how other people perceived me. The harsh reality I came to realize is, we can't fully control how other people perceive us. As much as I wanted the new leadership at the college to like me, I couldn't control their perception of me. It's not wrong to want a professor, classmate, colleague, or boss to like you. Just know, you can't *make* them like you if for some reason they don't. But you can be yourself. As I previously mentioned I've learned the hard way that I'm not everyone's cup of tea, but thankfully, to some I'm a glass of champagne.

Leading with confidence means leading from a place grounded in self-trust. I wanted the new leadership at the college to like me. I wanted them to believe I was capable and knowledgeable. So instead, when I saw how they treated people who disagreed with them, I was willing to change myself to become their version of the "perfect VP." Day in and day out, I wore my chameleon cloak. I was willing to have flexible, inauthentic boundaries and people-please. Although I thought this would keep me safe, these behaviors were slowly draining me. When I tried to manage the new leadership's perception, I slowly began to lose myself. Then, when I finally started showing up as my authentic self, I couldn't stay in that job any longer. Instead, I found my place in leadership coaching and keynote speaking.

Yes, we all want to be liked and feel like we belong. However, you can't change everything about yourself to feel that way. You are enough as you are now. If you don't feel accepted in one space, perhaps it's time to consider or capitalize on finding another place that will accept and celebrate you. When we continue to try to manage how others perceive us, we're presenting a warped version of who we really are. You'll always be asking yourself, "Do they like me?" Or, "Am I enough?" A healthy community will love you and know you're more than enough and communicate that back to you. The best way to find the people who will appreciate you is to consistently show up as yourself.

## IT'S DIFFERENT FOR WOMEN

I've had countless conversations with the women I work with as well as the women I coach surrounding leading with confidence. As with emotional intelligence, so much of it goes back to how we were socialized. While men are often taught that dominance is confidence, women are encouraged to blend confidence, collaboration, and empathy from a young age. Of course, being collaborative and empathetic isn't wrong, but women often are penalized for this when considered for leadership positions. I see this with many of my clients.

Through systemic bias, lack of representation, and internalized self-doubt, women have been told to live small. We have been told to be agreeable with a situation and to wait for the "right" time to do something. Although I encourage using discretion, there isn't always going to be a perfect time to ask for something you want. Often in these instances, my clients are asking for something they have deserved for quite some time. They share concerns like, "I know I have the skills, but I freeze in front of my colleagues." "I'm afraid of looking stupid." Or, "I'm worried they'll realize I don't belong there." These are vulnerable fears, and I understand. I have felt similarly at points in my life. Leading with confidence isn't leading without fear. It's choosing to be yourself even though you are afraid. Leading with confidence can be overwhelming, but don't give up.

# THE SABOTEURS AND THE WAY OUT

Although there are many practices that hinder confidence, perfectionism and people-pleasing are the prime saboteurs of confidence. People-pleasing encourages you to never say "no" so you'll always be accepted. And perfectionism tells you, "You're never good enough." Both corrupt confidence and plant fear in your mind. These saboteurs encourage you to carry them throughout your day under the lie that they will keep you safe. Instead, they are trapping you in a cycle of fear, shame, and despair. If you find yourself relating to either of these saboteurs, know that you are not alone. You are also more than the thoughts and behaviors you struggle with.

People-pleasing and perfectionism are masks we wear or have worn to feel safe, and it can be scary to try and live without them. But you can beat the saboteurs of confidence. Let me be clear—it's okay to be scared. Living in those mindsets may feel like it has protected you so far, but it won't forever. If you're living in fear, it's time to make the change to live in freedom. You don't have to live in the cycle. There are ways out! Let's walk through the steps to leading with confidence through Chessa's story.

## AWARENESS

Chessa was sitting in a meeting with a couple of supervisors when she thought of a great idea for the upcoming marketing meeting. Instinctively, she wrote it down and didn't give it another thought. Chessa was in the habit of shrinking herself, ever since a supervisor told her she needed to "think before she speaks." This interaction made Chessa feel like she was no longer in a psychologically safe environment.

Later that day, she went to therapy. There, she shared her thoughts, and her therapist asked her, "Why are you shrinking yourself?" Chessa was taken aback. She didn't believe she was shrinking. She believed she was protecting herself. After some journaling, she realized she was living in fear instead of leading with confidence. After speaking with her therapist, she was encouraged to practice a confidence check-in.

In moments where it's hard to know if you're shrinking or leading with discretion, a confidence check-in can help you. Let's do one together. Take a moment and ask yourself the following:

- Did I speak up for myself today?
- Did I hold or break a boundary?
- Did I celebrate at least one win today?

After checking in with herself for a couple of days, Chessa was ready to reframe her mindset to better lead with confidence.

## Reframe

Chessa needed to replace her self-doubt with confidence. She needed to believe she was capable of speaking up, even though her inner critic was telling her the opposite. The first step to reframing her mind was breaking through various confidence myths. Society tends to tell us that confidence looks like being extroverted or potentially arrogant. Chessa believed she wouldn't be able to lead with confidence since she was naturally more introverted. The truth is that confidence is choosing to act out of a place of self-trust. She needs to start living in a mindset based on "I'll try" over "I can't."

What mindset have you been living in? Think of a situation where you have said, "I can't," and replace it with something you can try. For Chessa, she decided to try speaking up for herself in the upcoming meeting.

## Action

When you're ready to take action, feel free to choose a big or small step—just be bold either way. Although Chessa was resolved to speak up in the upcoming meeting, she wasn't ready to share her ideas with the team leads. Instead, she decided she would give verbal affirmation to at least one question in the upcoming staff meeting. Remember, small wins build on themselves. Start from wherever you feel most comfortable.

Taking action can also look like being willing to say "no" to a request. This small practice can still build your confidence muscle. Sometimes, my mom will bring a dessert over to my house. My mom is a giver, and I know that's how she likes to show love—with food. When I was living in fear, I always said "yes" to whatever dessert she brought. Now, I lead with confidence and feel comfortable saying "no" when I don't want the brownie.

During keynotes, I always ask the audience to turn to their neighbor and say, "No." It's a request usually met with laughter, but by the end of it, the air in the room has shifted for the better. Where can you practice saying "no"?

## Reflection

When trying something new, it's important to understand how it made you feel. This is especially true when you're trying to grow your confidence. For Chessa, she journaled about how she felt when she spoke up in the last meeting. Initially, she felt elated and proud of herself. Great! Unfortunately, she later started to feel—as author and researcher Brené Brown would put it—a "vulnerability hangover."

Vulnerability hangovers happen when you feel discomfort after vulnerably sharing your preferences or truth. In those moments, it's important to confront the fear fueling the hangover with what's true about the situation. Things like those feelings are real and honest. The action you took is better than inaction. You'll do better next time. The more you try, the closer you will be to finding what makes you feel confident. Eventually, you will start reinforcing behaviors, and repetition is key to leading with confidence.

## Repetition

For six months, Chessa practiced leading with confidence. Now, she feels more than comfortable speaking up during meetings, and she feels ready to share her ideas with the rest of the team. Sure, Chessa still feels a little scared to share, but now she isn't stopped by fear. She trusts herself to speak, and she is ready to achieve her dream. The more Chessa practices self-confidence, the more confident she will become. Confidence is like ivy. As you care for and tend it, the more it will cover. And while it's great that Chessa is ready to share her wonderful ideas with her team, the real success is her consistent confidence. Whether her boss says "yes" or "no," she knows her worth and is grounded in who she is.

I've walked with many clients through fears like Chessa's. The women who are more than qualified, capable, and ready, but who are living in fear. After walking through the steps, I have seen clients' eyes light up as they tell me they got the job they were initially scared to apply for. I feel honored to be able to celebrate with them in those moments. Sadly, I've also had clients tell me how their voices were silenced when they bravely stood up for themselves. It's important to realize that leading with confidence doesn't mean you'll always achieve exactly what you want, but speaking up for yourself will lead you closer to the life you want to live.

## START NOW

Throughout this book, we have looked at the root of various issues like people-pleasing, emotional intelligence, and burnout. Now, you can reconstruct the foundation of what you believe. It's time to stop living in fear and lead with confidence. Every day, you're faced with the choice to either lead with confidence or live in fear. You don't have to wait for the right time, circumstance, or situation to change your life for the better. You can start doing a confidence check-in, writing in a brag book, or reaching out to a leadership coach for help. It's time to start trying some of these different confidence practices and finding what you like. Throughout my journey, I've found sharing my triumphant, flawed, and vulnerable stories is how I like to lead with confidence. When Harper looks at me with a giant smile and says, "Mom! You're a new you!" I feel affirmed that not only am I living in confidence, but I am also being the representation I've always wanted to see. It's never too late to start, but it's always better to just start now. So, start! You've got this!

# NOTES

# ACKNOWLEDGMENTS

**THERE IS NO** such thing as a self-made woman. This book carries the fingerprints of so many people who loved me, challenged me, and believed in me long before I fully believed in myself.

First, to my parents: Mom and Dad, thank you for teaching me truly unconditional love. You did your absolute best with what you had, and I see that more clearly now than ever. I am so grateful that I chose to be your daughter. Watching you now as grandparents is one of my greatest joys. Your love has been my foundation.

To my granny: You are the backbone of our family. A force. A steady strength. The summers I spent with you shaped me more than you will ever know. Your wisdom, your grit, and your belief that there are always ten more doors when one closes still guide me today.

To Anne, my editor and dear friend: What a full circle moment this is. From neighbor, to coworker, to friend, and now the one helping shape my words into something worthy of the world. You have supported me in every season, and I am deeply grateful for your steady presence and your belief in this message.

To all of my friends who have come in and out of my life: Each of you taught me something. Some stayed. Some were for a season. All mattered.

To Danielle, my bestie: I will never forget the moment we looked across the room and just knew. Instant friends. You have seen every version of me. You have walked with me through the highs and the heartbreaks. You have reflected back parts of myself I could not see. You just get me in a way that is rare and sacred. Thank you for always being there.

To my coaching friends and the women who took the time to read this book: We rise together. The conversations, the masterminds, the voice notes (Elyse, I cherish your voice notes and friendship more than words can express), the vulnerability. This work is not meant to be done alone. I am better because of you.

To my clients and audiences who have listened to me speak: Thank you for trusting me with your stories, your careers, your confidence. You are the reason this book exists. You are living proof that when women stop shrinking, everything changes.

To my daughters, Harper Jean and Lauren Rose: Your little souls and big personalities are why I do this work. You are watching. You are listening. You are learning what it means to be a confident woman in this world. I hope you always remember that no one gets to steal your joy or your voice.

To my husband, Ryan: You are my person. Thank you for loving me exactly as I am. For seeing me. For supporting every risk. For calming me when my dreams feel too big and cheering me on when they become reality. Your steady love and belief are woven into every chapter of this book. I am honored to be Dr. Kasi Lacey, and even more honored to be your wife. Thank you for loving a confident, loud Texan who never stops dreaming.

And finally, as cheesy as it may sound, I want to thank myself.

To my younger self, who knew there had to be a better way and kept pushing forward.

To the sixteen-year-old girl who moved out on her own and still filled out college applications.

To the college student who chased psychology like it was oxygen, who went on to graduate school, took on enormous student debt, and believed one day she would make an impact.

To the woman who fought tirelessly in her career, advocated for others, survived a toxic workplace, and walked away when her values were no longer aligned.

*It was not your fault.*
*You did not imagine it.*
*You were never too much.*

Thank you for surviving.
Now we are thriving.
This is your confidence comeback.

# ABOUT THE AUTHOR

**DR. KASI LACEY** has dedicated her career to helping women create lives and careers rooted in confidence, authenticity, and purpose.

As a psychologist, she spent years walking alongside individuals navigating life's most complex challenges. Through her clinical work and executive leadership roles in higher education, she developed a deep understanding of how confidence, mindset, and psychological safety shape the way people show up in their work and relationships.

Today, Dr. Lacey is an executive leadership coach, keynote speaker, and founder of H & L Legacy Consulting. She works with women and organizations across the country, teaching practical, psychology-based strategies to build confidence, prevent burnout, foster psychological safety, and lead with authenticity. Drawing from her experience as a psychologist and former C-suite executive, her work blends research, real-world leadership experience, and powerful storytelling to help others reclaim their voice and step fully into their potential.

Dr. Lacey is especially passionate about supporting high-achieving women who feel undervalued, stuck, or uncertain in their careers. Through her coaching, speaking, and writing, she equips women with the tools to overcome imposter syndrome, advocate for themselves, and create sustainable success without sacrificing their well-being.

A Texan at heart with strong Midwest roots, Dr. Lacey now lives in Missouri with her loving husband Ryan, their two daughters Harper Jean and Lauren Rose, and their beloved pups, Lane and Delta Dawn. When she is not speaking, coaching, or writing, you can often find her cheering on her daughters, reflecting on life on their growing farm, or dreaming up new ways to help women lead boldly and unapologetically.

# ENDNOTES


1 Dr. Gary Chapman, www.5lovelanguages.com

2 Gloria Wilcox, "The Feeling Wheel: A tool for Expanding Awareness of Emotions and Increasing Spontaneity and Intimacy," *Transactional Analysis Journal* 12, no. 4 (1982): 274–276. DOI: 10.1177/036215378201200411

3 Brené Brown, *Daring Greatly: How the Courage to Be Vulnerable Transforms the Way We Live, Love, Parent, and Lead* (Gotham Books, 2012).

4 Daniel Goleman, *Emotional Intelligence: Why It Can Matter More Than IQ* (Bantam Books, 1995).

5 Sheryl Sandberg, *Lean In: Women, Work, and the Will to Lead* (Alfred A. Knopf, 2013).

6 Jonathan Mond, et al., "Quality of life impairment associated with body dissatisfaction in a general population sample of women," *BMC Public Health* 13 (2013): 920. DOI: 10.1186/1471-2458-13-920

7 Diego Augusto Santos Silva, et al., "Prevalence and associated factors with body image dissatisfaction among adults in southern Brazil: A population-based study," *Body Image* 8, no. 4 (2011): 427–431. DOI: 10.1016/j.bodyim.2011.05.009

8  Dianne Neumark-Sztainer, et al., "Weight-control behaviors among adolescent girls and boys: Implications for dietary intake," *Journal of the American Dietetic Association* 104, no. 6 (2004): 913–920. DOI: 10.1016/j.jada.2004.03.021

www.ingramcontent.com/pod-product-compliance
Lightning Source LLC
Chambersburg PA
CBHW062145150726
47991CB00006B/2179